Soulbalance
Spiritual self-healing for the life of your Dreams
Hans Thörn Durefelt with Martina Thörn Durefelt

Second Edition

www.hansmartinatwinflames.com

ISBN 978-91-86889-20-3

Contents

Introduction

Chapter 1
The Key to Self-Healing p. 6

Chapter 2
The Five levels for a life in Balance p. 23

Chapter 3
The Soulbalance Method p. 49

Chapter 4
Your inner Truth p. 71

Chapter 5
Let your Intuition Guide you p. 96

Chapter 6
The importance of being Confirmed p. 115

Chapter 7
How to Make your Paradigm shift p. 128

Chapter 8
The Universe is with you p. 161

Chapter 9
To Grow as a person p. 175

Chapter 10
You are Unique p. 204

Chapter 11
The Way out of stress, depression, and phobias p. 219

Chapter 12
Live your Dream p. 249

Introduction

In today's society we have learned to create good self-esteem through things in life. Balanced self-esteem, the belief that we are good enough regardless of what happens outside of us, is, however, scarce. My name is Hans Thörn Durefelt, and I am the creator of the method presented in this book. I know well the importance of self-esteem. I have fought with poor health most of my life. I have lived with severe anxiety, been seriously ill, have a child with Down syndrome, and have been unemployed. But I've now gone through this pain and want to share what I've learned with other people.

My family was well off financially, and on the outside it certainly looked as if I had everything in place in my life when I was growing up. But my parents could not give me the love and support I needed, and by the time I was in my teens, I started to feel really bad. On the surface I was successful, both in sports and in school, but deep inside I felt worse then ever. When I was twenty years old, it had gone so far that I lay in fetal position in the apartment nearly all day, and I frequently drank too much alcohol. But because both physicians and psychologists found that there was nothing wrong with me, I continued with my life—without having received an explanation as to why I felt so bad. I got a bachelor's degree, earned a master's degree in marketing in the United States, and began working in multinational companies in different positions, even though I had severe anxiety.

In the mid-nineties, I could not handle it anymore—I broke down completely. I first went to the doctor and psychologist again, without being helped. Then I tried mental training, various health treatments, kinesiology, healing to process events from my childhood, and affirmations, but none of this helped me feel better. It was not until I took courses in deeper emotional and spiritual development, during which I began to establish contact with God and develop an intuitive feel of what was wrong in my life, that I began to feel better. This contact was not natural by itself, but was the product of all the suffering I had endured. I was initially extremely critical and wanted scientific proof of everything. But the spiritual and soul way was the only thing I had not tried, so I figured I had nothing to lose, since none of the other methods had helped me. I had come to the point where my soul was ready to help me to have a dignified and balanced life. First I was dejected; I felt that my life no longer had a sense of purpose. In despair, I was faced with a choice: I could give up life in full, or trust myself in God's hands. I had lived through giving up as long as I could remember, so I tried to just open myself to God's guidance.

At first, I used a method called kinesiology as a tool in my work—by pressing an outstretched arm and asking yes-or-no questions, I could read the response in the arm as strong or weak. After a while I realized that I could ask questions that were concerned with more than physical health. I began to get answers to questions relating to the world, the soul, and God, and I continued on that path. Eventually I did not need to do the muscle test; I just asked yes-or-no questions and got answers directly. Suddenly I got more and more access to the divine—I was simply guided by God and invited to create a new method in an entirely new direction. My confidence has now been strengthened to such an extent that I know that I can trust God in all situations. Today I use my contact with God to help others to heal and grow through their intuitive contact with God. I work successfully with coaching individuals to become spiritually in balance and achieve success in all areas of life.

In recent years I have helped over a thousand people, both in Sweden and abroad, to a happier and more balanced life using the method. What I want to achieve by writing down my message in the form of a book is to guide you in how you can make contact with your intuition, heal the damage you have, and create a happy life. This is the new spiritually guided coaching. A coach can never know what is right for a client. I would like to teach you how to use this method using your own intuition to guide you during your quest for inner and outer balance. Then magical things will happen. I know this after testing my method with great success on thousands of my clients.

Chapter 1

The Key to Self-Healing

During a child's upbringing, there are many needs that must be satisfied. We know that it is not enough to simply provide shelter, good food, and clean clothes. For a child to grow up to be a whole person who can live life fully and realize his or her full capacity, the child needs love and encouragement and a whole set of other emotional confirmations. Most of us did not get exactly what we need during our upbringing. This deficiency can appear as low self-esteem, anxiety, or difficulty in building and maintaining close relationships, among other things. It can also manifest itself as financial problems, an inability to handle success or setbacks, or anything else that prevents us from getting the life we really want.

Many of us have grown up with passive parents who may have put all their energy into a job or something else instead of their parenting responsibilities. It is often not what our parents *have done* but what they *have not done* which has caused us harm. This passivity has often been with our families through generations, as a kind of inherited paradigm which will result in such patterns as low self-esteem, feeling the lack of love, pain, and stress-related illness which repeats itself again and again. It is often said that there are personality traits that are genetically inherited in the family, but mostly it's just a negative, inherited paradigm which creates problems. If we as parents think that giving our baby everything it needs means buying nice clothes or going on a luxury trip abroad, then we are deceiving both ourselves and others by not giving our children the deep, unconditional love they need. Other examples of inaction may be that you do not stand up for your children and defend them in all situations, such as maltreatment in relationships with other adults, such as a teacher, or someone the same age. Not to love and support your children actively with words and actions when they choose their road in life, even if the child goes against the lifestyle you have chosen yourself, is also a passive way to lower your child's self-esteem.

In varying degrees, we have nearly all *received* what we do not need. It is not because our parents wanted to harm us, but because most of the parents carry various forms of shortcomings, sometimes deliberately but most often unconsciously, which then are passed on to the child. It is very difficult for a child to create better self-esteem, finances, health, and relationships than their parents because children usually take over their parents' habitual patterns. But it is never too late to repair these shortcomings. Anyone can do it. What is needed is a strong willingness to be open to change, to grow as a person, not only for oneself but for the sake of future generations. The seriousness with negative paradigms is that if the soul has been taught to see limits, say, low self-esteem, as a truth, it would not matter what your mind thinks of this; the feeling remains negative until the soul has created a different truth, your internal real truth, free from your negative paradigm and other people's harsh words. So it is not enough that you understand your limits—in this case, your lack of self-esteem—but you need to intuitively change your negative internal belief system, which has been built up by other people's opinions or actions against you, to really be able to grow into the person you want to be with unlimited self-worth and self-esteem.

It is possible to change these belief systems, which often are so deeply rooted in our soul that we perceive them as the truth. The child does not have a low self-esteem or phobias when it is born, but through the guardians' view of life during a child's youth and adolescence, the belief system that allows such negative patterns gradually emerges as the child nears adulthood.

The soul has endurance and is capable of a negative pressure from both the inside and the outside. But when the pressure gets too high, the soul's belief system is overwhelmed, and you get a person who is experiencing a life in chaos. Often, this takes as long as –fifteen to twenty-five years, but it can happen both earlier and later than that. Frequently excessive external and internal controls develop in this situation as the person attempts to relieve the pain of the soul. Unfortunately it is not until we actually solve our inner soul challenges that balance can be re-created and we can get rid of phobias, fears, the need for control, and other restrictions.

The Method that heals the Wounds

Soulbalance is a unique method that trains you to use your intuition to find the paradigms from your past that cause your current problems in your life. Once you have identified them, you can, with the help of God's power, heal the wounds of your soul. The search for the negative paradigms is done on five different levels (which we will return to): the spiritual, the soul, the emotional, the mental and the physical levels. The method is not limited only to finding and healing injuries from our childhood, as some of us perhaps have unexplainable symptoms resulting from traumas in previous lives. It can be necessary to heal these for you to get the life you deep-down want and have the spiritual capacity to create. A paradigm from past lives can affect you just as negatively as if it happened right now, because the soul is like a large database with endless memories. It can include everything from less serious occurrences to violent assault. The soul needs to understand and be enlightened for healing to happen. The method can of course also be applied to traumas occurring in adulthood, and even what is happening here and now. For some this book will undoubtedly act as a method of healing childhood traumas, and for others it will be a complete spiritual journey of discovery. Apply the book to your needs for optimal results. To write the book with such an open spiritual orientation is a choice I made to give each individual the best opportunity to heal. If I only address paradigms from this life, then all those that have traumas from past lives will not get the help they need.

I usually assert that we should be open to receiving help from others, but that we ourselves should make the crucial decisions about what we want or what direction to go in this life. When you decide in this way, you automatically become ultimately responsible for your life, instead of living for the norms and values of others. You are the only one who knows exactly what your intuition and your soul wants, so why let others make your decisions? The individuals who are most in balance are the ones that, in adulthood, take responsibility for their decisions and behavior. You are then true to yourself, and no one can take this attitude for life away from you unless you allow it. I have chosen to make all my final decisions intuitively, allowing me to build up my self-confidence more and more. If you like to help others, the best gift to give someone is the ability to build his or her confidence and feeling of self-responsibility. The inner pride increases in all individuals who can take care of themselves and their decisions, but to be the puppet of someone does not give you what you want, no matter how much others want to help you.

To become and stay in balance, you cannot rely on others indefinitely. There comes a time when you must decide for yourself what to do with your life, regardless of what others have in mind. When I coach individuals, we come to a point where they do not need to have advice and support from me on how to act. That is when their own intuitive soul power takes over. Sometimes I remind them that it is time, but usually the client knows that he or she is ready to create his or her own life. You can also add your own touch on how to use the Soulbalance method as long as it works for you. It's not as if you were to follow a strict diet that provides all the answers, because you know it never works to trust completely in others. Sure, strictly short term, the plan can work, but eventually the undermining, controlling paradigm will surface, sending you back to square one without asking your permission. Here you should just learn to trust yourself and not panic over what is right or wrong.

Creation Energy

The Soulbalance method works with the constraints encountered in previous lives, during adolescence, and in our adult lives. The book also highlights the creation energy, which I see as the time before there was visible life. Many of us also have links to that time, when the basis for the earth and the universe was created. When the earth was created, it all started with an energy source, the creation energy. God, who is the intelligence behind this energy, had access to only one creation energy cell. From this one energy cell arose everything on this earth has since that been created, including matter, plants, animals, and humans. Some of us have energy blockages from that time. There we can often find the cause of the extreme existential anxiety that many suffer from, and that neither the regular health care providers nor the religions have tools to solve. This anxiety is really an external symptom for us to learn to understand who we are, where we come from, and what a huge part, on a cellular level, we all have in everything created. Everything and everyone comes from the same creation energy cell, which in turn means that we all have the ability to reconnect with that original creative energy and therefore be involved in our healing, even on a cellular level. The only one that can and has the ability to create internal self-healing in yourself is you, which should not be seen as a burden but as an opportunity for a very special contact between you and God.

Everything that has been created on earth is related to God, either directly or indirectly—things created by humans, such as shoes, cars, houses--and to animals, plants and nature's own ability to create. We always bear God within us, in our soul, as we all come from God, and thus we have access to God's healing and creation at all times if we follow our intuition. I am throughout the book going to refer to God in a nonreligious sense, partly because that is how I see God, but also to give a healing tool that can reach many more beyond the boundaries of a religion or atheism, the choice not to believe in anything, which is like a religion in itself. But we all believe in one way or another, and atheists often have the same benefit from my method if they choose to believe in some form of universal power which science cannot explain. The book can also be read by a true skeptic, which I was before I discovered how accurate the Soulbalancing is. You may not even be interested or understand the spiritual level of healing. That is fine. The purpose of the book is to help as many people as possible with their healing process. Only you can determine what you need to help yourself heal through the Soulbalance method.

In many cases, one can say that the believers, especially those who do not belong to any religion, are allowed to be exposed to any type of critic, which no other group would have to endure without government interference. Therefore, many hide this spiritual side, in order not to be the joke of others' shortcomings on this subject. But just because science says you need scientific evidence does not mean that you do something wrong if you believe in God's healing power. I have met so many people who have found themselves in a nonscientific way. Have you, I, or anyone else the right to take that away from those who believe in something that cannot be proven scientifically? For those of us who know the internal pain of not being able to come out with our spirituality, there's really only one way to heal, and that is to dare to come out, regardless of what others think of it. I have often had to be sneaky with my spirituality in order not to offend others. With this book I put an end to that, and I hope it inspires you to really be what you want to be, regardless of what others think about you. I think that the soul and spiritual challenges are increasing for every generation, while our faith is reduced. Lots of people, including many children and young people, feel unsatisfied with life and are starving for soul and spiritual nourishment. I want to show that spirituality is not just for those who go to church or those who believe in the new age movement, but rather a necessity for a balanced life. Not that we have to be spiritual, but because, deep down in the soul, we long for the insight that we all are connected with everything and everyone.

It is time to show that the soul's connection to the universe is here to stay. Many think that spirituality belongs to the past, especially the kind of spirituality which has strong links with the world's religions. God, according to my insights, is an energy that is the power behind everything that has been created. By going back and intuitively finding what is limiting us, we can ask God what we need to do to become and be in balance. All individuals can do this by themselves, and it is therefore not necessary to go through a religion, if that is not the choice you make. I see myself as a believing atheist, where I believe in the power of God, but where I do not have to be in a special way to be worthy of contact with God. God is there to guide us and is extremely flexible and forgiving. For us to be in balance and get the life we want, and allow others the life they want, completely free of ego power, it is of decisive importance that we as individuals and as peoples strengthen both our internal faith (faith in ourselves) and our external faith (belief in God). Since everything is created by God, we need to believe in the divine power in order to become balanced and get a healthy planet.

Intuition and Healing

We have received two major abilities from God: an intuitive ability, which we can use to get the true answers we need, and a healing ability, by which God indeed helps us restore the inner spiritual balance. We will explore these possibilities and tools throughout the book. The challenge I will give you is that you should learn how to keep the intuitive power and the healing power open at all times. It always has to do with your self-image if you have difficulty finding your intuition. So the better self-esteem you create, the better the chance that you get your intuition to work. You also need to review your trust in God, for if it is weak, then the intuition will not survive. To keep the healing power open, you only really need the faith in God. This may sound both simple and difficult, and I have struggled many times with my negative paradigms to really understand that it is so simple, yet so difficult. What makes the Soulbalance method unique is that you can learn to intuitively find exactly what your soul needs to heal.

Let's say you have discussed a childhood trauma with a therapist, but no healing takes place. It has happened to me and many of my clients also. Say then that instead, your intuition guides you to the exact location in which the trauma is locked. Then inner healing spontaneously will occur, because you now have God's guidance to help you see objectively how your situation really is on an energy level, which is of major importance for your balance in life. Only God has this ability, and God is always there for you, whatever paradigm you have. It is not until you know that the trauma has lost its negative power in the soul that healing can take place. Nobody else has the ability to do this for you other then you in your relationship with God, so it's your own intuitive insights that will start the healing. The Soulbalance method helps you to access your unique intuition, which is the key to self-healing. Personally, I now live fully in harmony and accordance with my intuition and make all my decisions based on its guidance. Once I made the decision to fully rely on my intuition, really big miracles began to happen. I have let go of the ego, although it may not always look so to the outer world. Since that day a few years ago when I started to get guidance from God, I have not made an important decision against my intuition at all. In this way, I have reinforced my intuition and my contact with God more and more, and this can obviously also be true for you, if it is the path you choose.

Everyone can practice his or her intuitive abilities and get more out of life. By developing our intuition, it becomes easier to identify and heal the traumas we have. Through the Soulbalance method, you get access to exactly what you need for optimal healing and guidance. God will support you through better and worse, but keep in mind that healing often occurs when everything looks completely hopeless. Pain that is trapped in your soul must be released for you to be whole, and therefore a healing crisis may be exactly what you need. Welcome, therefore, the feelings you experience when you heal, no matter what you are experiencing. Actually, it is only our society that has said that negative emotions should be hidden. The truth is that they must be experienced for healing to happen. When you follow your intuition, things fall into place in a way that can appear inexplicable. In fact, this only shows that the intuition works as a tool for you and me to bring us closer to our dreams.

The Soulbalance method is a way to heal your traumas, but it can offer you more than that. It can give you access to the special spiritual guidance that intuition opens you up for as we follow its path in life. Suddenly you achieve what you want, because your intuition sees opportunities where your paradigm sees obstacles. My advice to you is still not to use your intuition to try to see exactly what will happen in the future, for you will then lose one of life's greatest gifts, uncertainty. Without uncertainty we would not need faith, and without faith we would not be able to have our special relationship with God, which is based on trust and uncertainty. But you can, of course, use your intuition when taking a decision to do something or not. Intuition is then used more as a guide to help you find your true path in life, free from negative paradigms and the negative impact of others.

The Soul

To understand how we humans work, we must realize that the soul is the base for the body, and not vice versa. The soul is the foundation for everything in us, creating the meaning of life. There are really two ways to live. You can choose to live in a way that other people and society expect of you, without having contact with your soul, or to live and do what feels right for yourself, deep down in your soul. The meaning of life is discussed in a variety of books. The purpose of life is not to be happy. Many believe that if you are not happy, there is something wrong and that you are not good enough. But life is really about the soul trying to find answers for growth and balance. In the search you need both challenges and rewards. Happiness is actually a temporary condition which you can experience from time to time when you create balance in the soul. Overall balance is, however, a lasting experience. You can be sad or happy, but in the depth of your soul, you feel more and more full. Be careful not to put too much pressure on yourself when you seek balance. If you want to experience happiness all the time, you will be disappointed. The state is not permanent. But to be in balance, to be one with the soul all the time, that is to create the life you want. This quest includes both pain and happiness to help the soul grow to its full potential.

Inner Truth

Every child, every person, has a soul that needs different kinds of food to grow. We adults tend to form our children to what fits our standards and values, but these paradigms do not necessarily suit our children. Typically, our norms and standards are not even our own, but they come from our parents, who in turn got them from their parents. In the end, we do not live our inner truth, but instead live with a lot of ideas and habits without even knowing where they come from. Some people also have so many energy blocks from past lives and the creation energy that it does not matter how good a job the parents do, because the child will still feel unworthy and unfortunate. The knowledge of how to heal oneself intuitively means that there is now hope for all who struggle with their inner demons. For me the soul is the key to virtually everything in life. Life is not about just being nice, but above all being true to oneself in all aspects of life. When we follow our inner truth, the soul gets exactly what it needs for self-healing.

By "follow the inner truth," I mean to live after the internal intuitive guide that is deep within the soul. When we follow this guide, we live more and more in line with our inner truth, and we get better and better balance in life. Imagine that you are so formed by the opinions of others that you really do not know what is right or wrong for you. You live only to be good enough for others. It is not an especially rich life, but unfortunately it is a reality for many of us. If you then start to live by your inner truth, which you intuitively get from God, then nothing can stop you. It can be that your intuition will give you completely different answers than those you get from your thoughts. Remember that your inner truth is your truth, but your paradigm is the image that others have created for you. Unfortunately, it is often not true, and you may not have the life that you really want as long as you follow it. When we follow our inner truth, the ego no longer has power over us. We have created the ego because we are trying to do things that are good enough for others' opinions. They can be anything from showing off a huge house to bragging about all the millions of dollars we have. If we follow our inner truth, we may achieve the same external results, but we are not doing it to be good enough for others; we are doing it because we know that it is the path that is right for us.

The Five Levels

When I started creating the Soulbalance method, it was not my own invention; I developed it through a variety of "coincidences" that caused me to really rely on my contact with God. I have spent many days and nights questioning the answers God gave me, but every answer I got was in fact just what I needed. Now, you will have access to the contact I have with God, and I hope it will give you what you need. You may choose to call the universal power which I call God whatever you want; maybe the word "God" feels awkward and wrong for you. The force is not linked to any religion but is a universal power, without dogma. Based on the messages I have received through my contact with the universal power, I have divided our lives into the five levels that the Soulbalance method is based on. The method assumes that we all can get access to and are a part of the universal power (God). Through our contact with God, we all have the spiritual level of contact with the universal soul, which is God's channel of communication with us. The universal soul has the answers for every living being. It is our task to dare to trust our intuitive ability and actually make use of the universal soul's wisdom and power.

Every individual is connected to the universal soul through the individual soul. One could say that our soul is our direct contact with God and the universal soul. From this soul level, the divine healing spreads further to our emotions *(the emotional level)* and our thoughts *(mental level)* to finally manifest in physical performance *(physical level).* By having direct communication between the universal and our individual soul, we can bypass all the paradigms that our thoughts, feelings, and actions stand for to prevent us from growing. When the soul well gets the spiritual healing it needs, our approach to life will positively change automatically, creating our true potential through results in the external world. Sometimes the soul wounds are so deep that they even have caused serious, permanent changes in our way of thinking, feeling, and creating results. In these cases you also need behavior change exercises to really achieve what you want. Say, for example, that you resolve a phobia on the soul level. Then you need to also implement a deliberate, external behavioral change to make the positive, soul change permanent on all levels of life.

Insights for Balance

As we begin, it is good to have five insights about the process of achieving balance in life:

1. Never go, consciously or unconsciously, into submission and believe that you are worth less than anyone else. It is so easy to be put in a situation where you think you're worth less than someone else.

2. You do not need rituals to have contact with God. Many of us believe that we must live in a special way with rituals and through the church to be good enough for God.

3. There is no hierarchy in your communication with God. For someone else to say that he or she is closer to God than you, or that he or she has the right to decide what God wants for you, is not the path that God

wants to go. If you have your own honest relationship with God, then that is good enough, no matter what any spiritual leader thinks about it.

4. It is not necessary that you believe in God. It is enough that you believe there is a greater intelligence that can help you become a more complete human being. If you are uncomfortable with the word "God," use any other name that suits you better. God does not care what you call him or her. As long as you create an inner faith in something, anything is possible. God helps those who want to create a better world, even if they do not believe in God in a religious sense.

5. You do not need the approval of others to get help from God. There are certainly plenty of people who have other opinions than you, but regardless of what they think and no matter who they are, you are good enough in God's eyes.

With these sentences, I hope you get the insight you need that you are good enough, whatever your paradigm and whatever others think of you. There is hope in despair, and miracles do occur. Dare to trust that you are the one to determine what to do with your life, and you will sooner or later realize that you live your life in accordance with your inner truth. In the process of self-healing, you should always interact with your internal truth so that you know you are right on track.

We all have a true guiding principle that should work in all situations, but for some it has lost its significance. If your inner truth is not working properly, it can be rectified when you resolve your paradigm energy blocks. You will finally live your inner truth and have access to your intuition when you want to heal. When you are chasing and pushing to achieve something, it rarely works. The reason is that when you push yourself to achieve something without having learned the lesson of what stops you and what it means to you to solve this spiritual mystery, you will stand still even if you give it everything you've got. If you know deep inside that it will be okay, God will help you to achieve what you want. It may look really bad, but deep inside you will know that it will go well. The fear that will surface, you can then heal using the Soulbalance method. Basically, God always provides us with hope, faith, and support when we need them the most. With the help of your intuition, you can identify your issues, which for many otherwise would be lost in our intellectual way of living. There is always healing power under your paradigms, and everything can be solved no matter how impossible it looks on the surface.

Chapter 2

The five levels for a life in Balance

The creation of the Soulbalance method began when I took courses in personal development and, through them, I came in contact with a person who said I should get in touch with my soul in order to create balance. I started to evaluate many different spiritual methods, and through that the embryo to my unique coaching and self-healing method eventually emerged. At that time I did not believe in God at all, so it was a difficult process to establish contact. In my early childhood I actually had a strong belief in God, which both fascinated and scared my mother! Instead of receiving answers from her to my questions about God, I was ignored when mentioning God, probably because my mother thought it was uncomfortable to talk about a subject for which she had no answers. My way of trying to get my mother's approval was to avoid addressing God, and as a result of this I lost my belief in God entirely. Another event that made me not believe in God happened when I was five years old and we were living in England and a teacher threatened me that I would be punished by God. My mother later said that I turned off my feelings totally after that and never really became the same happy person as before. In this way, I became more and more turned off from God's power, which I unknowingly had repressed, while the divine really was the key to my healing and my strength in life.

Through the years of existential anxiety, I was looking for the answers but found them nowhere until the day I realized that the only possibility I had not tried as an adult was precisely the divine path. But I did not find God through meditation or in church, where many feel a sense of connection to the universal power. I found the contact with God by being completely open-minded and full of trust and just starting a dialogue with the universal power, which I began to believe was there, and seeing where the dialogue took me. I was in such bad shape that I let go of all illusions about how life should be. I gave up in a way, but by giving up and surrendering, I came in contact with the pure healing power of life. I let go of all thoughts that I must be in a special way to be good enough. I let go of the fear about material living, and I let go of my ego trying to live up to the expectations of others—not that I wanted to, but because I had no choice. I had reached a point in life where I had no other way to go.

Quite soon miraculous things started to happen with me and my family, and even my clients had the same healing experiences. I was totally convinced: God, whom I so long had been separated from, had found a place back in my life and heart. Actually, I am a messenger of something that is much larger than my mind can understand. Once I realized this and let go of my ego, more and more intuitive messages came from God. I reached the conclusion that healing is within us, in close contact with our intuition, which is our direct contact with God and the universe. To seek contact inward is the only way to achieve sustainable balance and success in life. No one else can really heal you. The answers to all your questions can only be answered by your intuition in close contact with

God. Our intuition is God's gift to humanity. This means that when we have faith, we can create what we want. The more true you are to yourself, the more you can enhance your intuitive and healing communication with God. You should not do this to be good enough for someone else, but because you know you need to walk your true path to heal yourself and others. Intuition, which is a strong sense that something feels right in both body and soul, often takes you in a direction different from what other people point out for you.

Once you start being true to yourself, positive things will start to happen to you and your relationship to the divine power. This does not mean that everyone will welcome the change, because who will now be someone's doormat when you leave that place behind? But when you are true to yourself, God will certainly support you in everything you do so that you can become what you are meant to be. If you're not there yet, it will surely come, so try to be forgiving when you make your so-called mistakes, as this is a great part of the healing to create balance in your life. For my part, the all-important decision to trust my intuitive power at all times led to the conclusion that I felt worthy for the first time in my life—worthy of myself and, above all, worthy in God's eyes! For the first time ever, I felt good enough. No other person had given me this gift of adequacy, and now it came directly from God. It was salvation for me, because I had really given up all hope of having any value at all. I was completely captivated, because I had no premonitions that God would confirm me in this powerful way. Even today, I am grateful for every second I may share part of God's gifts. This is more valuable to me than all the money in the world and can never be replaced. I thank you, God, for my life and the value you give it.

Insights for Healing

In the world I lived in, with a father who was a successful CEO and my own career in the international world, I met a lot of resistance when I chose to go down the spiritual path. When I first worked as a coach, I based my work on long-established coaching techniques that I had learned in various established coach training courses, both in the United States and Sweden. By that time I was feeling a bit better; I had moved home to Sweden and started to take care of my physical health and get in touch with my intuition. But the results for my clients and me were not as good as I had expected. And I still felt really bad at times. The contact with my mother was problematic, and I noticed how my own children were affected. It was not until I totally dared to start my dialogue with God and let go of my fears that things began to happen. Great stuff! My children's allergies disappeared, I could have contact with my mother without feeling bad, and my clients got fantastic results.

Through my contact with God, I came to the conclusion that we consist of five levels. The levels are the physical, the mental, the emotional, the soul and the spiritual (we will go into more detail about the levels later in this chapter). By intuitively exploring my own pain to the soul level, I identified my traumas and could heal them. The Soulbalance method is there to help us identify our injuries at the soul level and then letting God's healing power heal them. When it comes to our children, we can learn in depth what they need to avoid in order not to get traumas, and, to the extent they receive them anyway from us or others, help them to heal so the traumas lose their negative power to influence their lives. With the help of your intuition, you always start healing on the soul level. From the soul level you can then more specifically adapt the method so that it helps to change the mind-set, find new, positive emotional memories, and really change the external physical results for the better. When you follow this method, there are really no limits to what you can achieve. I have seen clients get healed from deep depression, get rid of phobias, and in some cases even get rid of allergies. I cannot determine what will happen to you, but your unique contact with God will give you the answers.

More about the Healing Creation Energy

I have used the Soulbalance method for several years, both in workshops where I help participants resolve trauma issues and as a coach for individuals and businesses. With my image, I can, on the surface, look more like a normal neighbor than a man who speaks with God, and this allows me to come in contact with people who might otherwise not have dared to look inward for a better quality of life. Many people I meet get a bit scared when I start talking about God, but when I go ahead and explain my view of God in general, practically everyone sees the whole picture. You might object that you do not believe in God, but when the universe was created there was only energy—the energy science calls the "Big Bang." God is the intelligence behind that energy, the intelligence behind the creation energy. Then, all cells, organisms, insects, animals, and humans evolved from it. This creation energy never disappears, and we are all connected to it. We can all trace our way back to the creation energy and heal the traumas we had on the way to where we are now. The creation energy is the gift of God and is completely disconnected from everything negative that happens on earth. Creation energy is available for all of us to use as long as we do it for a good purpose, namely, as long as our actions do not harm anyone or anything on purpose. And it is not possible to abuse creation energy since it only works when the user has positive action in mind. When you are out to harm others or boast your ego, you simply cannot access it.

To dare to let go

During the first year of using the Soulbalance method, I asked God questions, and I got answers all the time. I had full access to my intuition. But eventually I experienced long periods during which I was more or less forced to rely on God without intuitively being able to verify his existence. It was then that the true soul and spiritual growth in me took place. Being able to work intuitively, while I occasionally dared to let go and let God create all the magic without me involved, was incredibly challenging for me, as I had grown up with the need for having personal control, where all decisions had me involved. As a result, I had created a controlling habit to verify and reconcile all things with God. But God's intelligence and wisdom know what is best for both you and me, so I finally had no choice but to let go of the almost manic divine control needs I had when starting my intuitive journey. I wanted to be in balance with the method I created, so I had to let go of my doubts in God and thus my strong need to prove the existence of God and his healing power. My strong need for control meant that I wanted everything scientifically proven because of my fear of making mistakes or having my method considered a scam. But the more evidence I searched for, the worse I felt. To be able to become free and have access to the huge divine healing power, I had to let go of my internal and external fears.

The key is to know that God is with us no matter what our negative paradigms have taught us and regardless of what other people say or think. Now I know that at certain times the divine power will do what is best for me and the whole, and that I intuitively cannot get answers to my questions about this. In retrospect, I can then see how great this divine power is that often gives us solutions and opportunities that are far greater than what our minds have the capacity to understand. This insight solved many hang-ups for me and was the biggest reason why I could let go of so much of my internal and external control behavior. An excessive need for control is perhaps the most common cause for mental and emotional imbalance. It can manifest itself in that you are always perfect at work, you keep the home obsessively clean, or you are unable to be flexible when plans change. Really difficult, obsessive control behavior can be to repeatedly clean one's hands, or to need to repeatedly check that, for example, the oven is turned off. Often we have one or more controlling behavioral habits to hold our negative emotions at a distance so that they do not hurt us. Unfortunately, they harm us more when they are repressed in our subconscious mind. We tend to do everything humanly possible to avoid facing the feeling which is the root of the real underlying problem. When we try to escape from our true feelings, we often create a variety of secondary symptoms that do not really have anything to do with the real cause of the problem. When you then only treat the symptoms, you are never totally free.

With the Soulbalance method, I would like to help you get rid of the real causes for your pain rather than just treating the external symptoms. The symptoms can be anything from severe alcohol or drug problems to a nonrelaxed approach to food or exercise. How do you know when you have the kind of controlling behavior that conceals something else? If you cannot let go of a certain behavior without feeling anxiety, you are certainly a person with destructive control needs—not because of what you do (for example, run five miles a day), but because of the feelings that the controlling behavior suppresses. It is fantastic to work out, but if it is like a drug, there is an underlying healing potential for your behavior patterns, and when you free yourself from your control, you will feel balanced and free. In my own situation, there was a choice between losing the contact with God and maintaining my controlling behavior, or increasing my intuitive contact with God and daring to let go of my need for control—and the choice was really quite simple.

Since I was four or five years old I had felt that I was not good enough. I was full of negative behavioral patterns that controlled me and that had been created to relieve me from the underlying sense of despair and powerlessness that really wanted to come up to the surface. I hated myself so much that I created negative associations with everything I came in contact with, and I felt this self-loathing twenty-four hours a day. Since I was feeling bad at all levels, I became allergic to some food and electricity, for example. I could not be physically close to some people, and I created phobias for everything ranging from tight spaces to social situations. The feeling of self-loathing got attached to everything I did, and finally I was living in a controlled unlocked prison where no guards where needed but where my paradigms controlled me in all situations. When I later released and neutralized the negative emotions with the Soulbalance method, all the negative habits that gave fuel to my controlling behavior disappeared. It was my way of becoming free. The hard part is to dare to break the negative pattern and get rid of the negative emotions. We really need to discover who we are to become free, which is often the more frightening than continuing to live with suppressed emotions. We want so badly to have our feelings under control, but in this case it is the excessive control that keeps us away from a free and balanced life.

To dare to break my controlling paradigms, with all the resistance I was feeling, is probably the best but also the most challenging experience I have had. But since it has had such a direct, positive influence on me, and indirectly on all those I have helped, I am so grateful that I dared to take that step in the right direction. The more I have dared to grow and get closer to God, the more positive situations I have attracted, so more and more people have had access to this healing method. When you and I become free, we also motivate others to take that step.

The Contact with God

The five levels have come to me in my dialogue with God. They are the physical, mental, emotional, soul and spiritual levels. Everyone is in contact with all of the five levels, consciously or unconsciously. If there is an openness to change, healing can always take place, but a closed, skeptical approach does not help our self-healing potential. My insight that we are made up of five levels, and that we can trace the issues to the soul level and heal ourselves, revolutionized my life and the lives of my clients. I use the method to find the underlying cause of a problem that I or someone else has. It is a unique approach based on strengthening our intuitive ability and using it as a guiding tool. The intuitive ability comes from spirit (God) and then goes through your soul, your feelings, and your thoughts to finally manifest itself in physical results. It is our relationship to the universe, God, that determines our power on the spiritual and soul levels. It makes us humans unique.

We have the ability to be God's helpers and convert God's will into feelings, thoughts, and finally into physical form. You are actually an extension of God for what needs to be done on earth. God has given us the ability to express what he or she wants to do in physical form. But since the ego often takes over, many just do what is best for them. God wants us well, but the ego often wants unhealthiness to satisfy a bunch of false negative paradigms. Then there is no access to God, and then rather negative situations can be created, as in abuse, war, or bullying. We need to learn to understand the difference between these choices at all levels and in all situations. Were we, as individuals and as a group, able to understand how we can establish and maintain our relationship with God, much of the evil and wickedness in the world would cease to exist. How many wars are fought in God's name or the name of religion when the ego is really hiding behind this false act? If the false motives of these leaders were revealed, then in each country these individuals' power would be lost, and without power over the people, their often self-centered leadership would fade away. If there were no wars in the name of God, there would actually not be any wars at all. With regard to more local, individual violence, such as bullying, it would cease if each individual learned to follow his or her internal truth, which is our true connection to God. When we follow God through our inner truth, the ego loses its negative power and the negative circumstances cease to exist. This book's aim is to really help everyone to understand who or what God really is and stands for, and that we, with the Soulbalance method, can heal our wounds and create balance. In the long term this could create a free world. You can choose the divine path at all times. The choice is yours.

The Universal Soul

Deep inside, you have a connection to God which is the pure truth. This link between your soul and God is the universal soul. This links all people and all living things with each other. The universal soul has the answer to everything: what will happen, what is happening, and what has happened. It knows things that have not yet reached our conscious mind. An inventor can think and get answers from the universal soul on how he or she shall process an idea. One can ask questions of the universal soul about how to solve relationship and health problems.

This dimension is much larger than our intellect. We can connect with it when we need to solve problems we cannot cope with the usual way. The Soulbalance method helps you to establish this intuitive contact. You get an opportunity to find information related to you and your soul that will lead you to what you have to change to begin to live by your inner truth. Sometimes you may get surprising answers when you are using your intuition to connect to the universal soul. Since our individual soul constantly strives for balance, the answers you get can mean you have to deal with some uncomfortable things before you can enjoy balance in life. Sometimes things happen that we could not predict intuitively. Do not see this as a failure, but rather as a higher collective truth which comes from God even though you and I may not be able to see exactly how things have occurred or will occur. In my case, I have a child with Down syndrome, which is a handicap that everyone would like to avoid. But for me, it was indirectly the key to everything I stand for. Through having a child with a handicap, I realized I could try setting up a perfect facade, but I could not fool myself anymore. It was so obvious that I was not like others, so I decided to live life fully and have the courage to do what my paradigm said I did not know how or have the ability to do. Unfortunately I needed so much pain before I would wake up. If we had control over everything in every situation, whether by intuition or not, life's magic would cease to help and surprise us. If the intuitive power was so accurate at all times that it always could be proven, the belief in would God cease. We will not always know what to do, but we can learn to trust that the right thing will happen regardless of whether we know it intuitively or not.

Past Lives

Some need to dig deeper than others to achieve balance. This sometimes has to do with how many past lives they have lived. The people who have lived many lives often feel worse and have more difficulty getting help from traditional health care than others. We have created the idea of dividing the human condition into life and death, but the soul really is much more, regardless of condition. Sometimes much of what we need to solve occurred in a previous life, but everything is a hole for the soul and therefore affects us even in this life. The pain is large or small regardless of its origin, and the soul sees pain as pain, regardless of where and how it arose. When you learn to understand these challenges that often go unresolved from life to life, you will realize what you gain if you really solve what needs to be resolved.

The soul would like to create balance and develop you to be the best that you can be, but it carries soul memories to the next life. This means that what you do not solve in this life, you will have to solve in the next. Therefore, do some soul searching and identify your challenges so you can do the best you can in this life. When you heal yourself, it's like peeling an onion, where you go through layer after layer. You encounter a problem at a time, solve it, feel better, and then go on. The more you peel, the closer you are to your inner truth. And the closer to your inner truth you get, the more painful resistance you meet. Then it is up to you to dare to meet the traumas that you could not manage earlier. When you were on the outside of the peel, you could not see the stress that was sitting further in. Not to release all the pain at once is a way for the soul to protect itself, for it cannot handle solving all the issues at once. The pain will become progressively stronger the further in you go, but you will heal more and more, for you are taking yourself closer to your inner truth. Often this healing takes place alternately—layers of pain alternated with layers of calm. These two different states of mind are important for us to get the insights we need. To dissolve the pain by reaching inside brings you closer to your inner truth, while the balanced periods are important for retrieval and reflection. By becoming aware of this process, you know that you are on your way to heal yourself. Be your own guru and let no one decide or say what is best for you. At first, you will need some help along the way, but eventually your inner power and divine capacities will take over. You are now about to become free, a condition where you know what is right for you at all times.

The Five Levels

I will now in more detail describe the different levels you need to know to use the Soulbalance method of healing. All levels are linked to each other. God's healing power goes through the spiritual level (God) to our soul (intuition), so that new feelings and thoughts ultimately can translate into improved physical performance. The next chapter explains in detail how to use your knowledge about the five levels in order to achieve self-healing. This does not mean that you can only work with the intuition and the Soulbalance method with the framework that I describe. Eventually, your unique soul will create the conditions and answers that you specifically need. View the five levels more as a foundation for how each individual is linked to the universal soul, which ultimately is God's tool for communicating with us. You will be using your intuition to get the insights you need to find the soul cause of your limitations. The more you try controlling pain and stress which are blocked in the subconscious, the more limited results you get. This means that you are stuck in life, no matter what your external front says, and you will need to resolve your internal challenges to create balance. If you try to solve them using only the power of thought, you will not get the results you want. The blockages are like a puzzle that needs to be resolved correctly and in the correct order. The Soulbalance method does just that, which neither science nor our common sense can resolve. Therefore, it is no use trying to calm your emotions, and any type of training which does just that, such as mental training, meditation, or yoga, only functions when the system is clean from the cause of internal stress. But as soon as there is a single cause of stress, it needs first to be explored and solved in the soul before healing takes place. When you use the Soulbalance method, it gives you the effect you seek.

A - The physical level

On the physical level, you can see how your finances, your health, and your relationships are. The physical level is the external manifestation of the other levels. The reason why we feel uncomfortable or do not experience balance in life rarely has its origin on the physical level. Even with obvious symptoms—for example, you have a sore arm because you fell cycling and broke it, or you've got the flu or shopped too much—the reason for the problem is often on another level.

In order to achieve a lasting balance, you need to maintain and achieve balance in at least five areas on the physical level:

1. *Physical fitness.* If you do not take care of your physique through exercise, you unfortunately do not have 100 percent respect for yourself. Feeling good physically is as important as feeling good in the soul. Physical exercise takes you a step closer to your inner truth to you love

yourself unconditionally. If you do not have this in place, do not despair, for it can be solved. Decide now to be physically active on a regular basis, and you will be one step closer to your whole self.

2. *A healthy diet.* If you eat right, you give yourself the best fuel for a balanced life. The more balanced a diet you eat, the more respect you have for your own health. Select a path today that suits you so you get what you need in terms of food and drink.

3. *Financial health.* So many have money problems, and this can really create stress in all other areas. Many people claim that money is not important, but good financial health helps you build a foundation so you can relax and create balance in other areas. Sound finances are no guarantee for balance, but they are often one piece of the whole that needs to fall into place.

4. *Good sleep.* Sleep just enough, because too little or too much sleep diminishes your creative power. If you are constantly tired and listless, it might not be because you sleep too little; it could also be due to your sleep quality, which is about more than just the number of hours you sleep. Do you wake up refreshed? Then you got the sleep you need, whether you have slept three or ten hours.

5. *Self-fulfilment.* When you manifest your dreams into physical form (realize your true self), even on a physical level you automatically feel better. If you have a dream, realize it in physical form; otherwise you go against what your soul really wants, which gives two negative effects: a)

you do not achieve what you want; and b) you feel sick about not being true to yourself. This is perhaps the challenge which is written of the least in books on natural health. But when you are manifesting your dreams in physical form, you physically also feel better. To really get to do what one wants in life and to see the natural fruit of this is a healthy gift that not enough people have the pleasure to enjoy. Make sure you give yourself the opportunity to realize your dreams and create the life you really want right now. If you feel something in your physical life that you really do not want to have (for example, you live in a destructive relationship or have money troubles or poor health), you have the ability to heal the cause to all this with the Soulbalance method. But you must always make the decision to also manifest the change in physical form. You need to make sure that you really do what you are meant to do. If you resolve a trauma, you often need to take action to really implement the change. Say that you resolve a trauma that has to do with poor self-esteem. Then maybe your inner truth says that you really need to take that step to start the company which you have dreamed about during all these years. Without doing this, there will be no business, and you will feel bad that you are not being true to yourself.

B - The mental level

The mental level consists of your thoughts and how you express yourself. For some it may be sufficient to take a course in mental training to get through to the challenges arising from the mental level. Mental training is a great tool when the soul is in balance and free from negative blockages. But mental training used to run over underlying soul and spiritual challenges may alternatively have the opposite effect and

for you to be whole. To ignore these messages is often the biggest reason that life is not in balance on the soul, emotional, mental, or physical level. For example, if you feel you do not love yourself, and this is engraved in your paradigm, it is an experience on the emotional level. But the basic reason that you feel unloved may be traced to the soul level, looking specifically for balance with your inner truth.

There are really only two ways to experience negative emotions. One is that negative things happen that causes negative emotions, and these feelings are buried in the soul's database. The second is when you start to free yourself from the negative emotions that have been locked in the soul. Then you experience the exact same negative feeling as when the trauma was created. Relax in this process and let the emotions come out as a healing crisis. The difference between not having started your healing and really being in the healing process is that you are going to see flashes of hope and joy when you free yourself from the negative paradigms. By deciding to work on yourself, in this case by reading this book, you have taken a first step in the healing process. Unfortunately, traditional health care often misses this aspect in the decision process of how to treat patients. In a state of active emergency, traditional health care often has the resources you need at that moment, but when you heal, you need to allow the healing process to take care of the magic. It is good to know that if you have negative feelings stored in your subconscious, but try to think positive, you will only strengthen the power of the negative emotion. It may be that you are mentally positive about holding a lecture but emotionally scared, and when you then try to do well, you just reinforce the negative feeling you have inside you and get a bad result. The solution is to release the soul blockage so that the negative feeling does not produce the same symptoms over and over again. You now understand why the feeling was present in your life and that you do not need it anymore. It has given you the message and the lessons you need. Negative feelings repeat until you intuitively have found out why you have them, using the Soulbalance method.

D - The soul level

The soul is the intelligence you have in you when you are born. It is your link to the universe, which we call God. The soul comes to you about an hour before birth. There are two reasons for this. First, there must be a soul which is free for you, and then there is no reason to take decisions in advance. The second is that God knows what challenges your soul needs to grow to its full potential. In my case, I had exactly the parents I needed, with all the pain it took to grow into who I am today. Without these challenges, which in my case were life-threatening, I would never have learned life's mystery: that life is about growing, challenging oneself, daring to be the one you should be no matter how scared you are. Your soul can be completely different from the other souls in the family you are born into, which can mean just the right challenges for you. You have to dare to commit yourself to become what you are destined be, irrespective of whether the rest of the family agrees with you or not. The soul just reflects how much your life is in balance with your inner truth. Your soul is like a database full of positive and negative memories that you sometimes know and sometimes do not know, but they are still there to guide you to balance. The largest challenges exist in the soul, something that often modern science has missed—not that the challenges are not there, but because science has no tools to prove their existence yet.

As I mentioned earlier, the soul always intuitively seeks answers so that you get to live your inner truth, the life you really want and are able to have. My question to you now is: What is your inner truth? Each individual is unique, and we are born to enrich ourselves and others. Your inner truth knows exactly what you are meant to do. But if you live in accordance with the paradigm you received during your childhood, it is not at all certain that you are living according to your inner truth. This may mean that you do something that you think is right on a physical level, but not on your soul level. It is because of this that some people are burned out, depressed and may have stress-related illnesses. Then you must have the courage to change direction and trust the intuitive connection to the soul, which is your link to God. The soul wants to have long-term balance while the ego wants short-term thrills. The ego often uses alcohol, drugs, obsessive eating, destructive sex, the wrong attitude towards money and power abuse, trying to keep the paradigms where you feel you have to be good enough to be happy. The question is, what do you need to do to live a full life without restrictions? The truth is quite simple, but difficult for most people to take in: Be true to yourself, transform your limitations to opportunities, challenge your limiting fears, have the courage to change, and trust your intuition. When you do this, you do not need the destructive, negative ego habits anymore. Destructive behavior is often a way to keep negative emotions in check by ignoring or distracting them.

E - The spiritual level

The spiritual level is God outside us. At this level you have the universal soul. All humans, animals, and other living things are linked with each over on the soul level. The universal soul knows the truth about what happened, what will happen, and what is happening right now. When someone receives a real super idea—for example, invents something great—they have had contact with the universal soul. It sends you intuitive truths so you can live your inner truth. You do not have to belong to a religion to get access to the universal soul; the channel is open whether you believe in God or not. When we do good things, such as helping someone else, it opens up the flow to the universal soul even more, and vice versa. This can be seen when one consider the people who make money through activities that benefit the world, compared to making money on selling drugs or weapons. The people who make money on an activity that creates misery will never be happy. If one builds richness on this type of activity, it can cause problems for several generations. The universal soul has all the answers; they are simply to trust your intuition, get connected, and rely on the answers you receive. You know you're on the right track when you get a positive feeling, enrich yourself and others, and get positive results.

Your Life Energy

I believe that our inner truth is our life energy and our power in life. When we are born, we have an open contact with our inner truth, but through the years of smothering paradigms from our parents and others around us, we often move farther and farther away from it. We are all born with an intuitive power within us, but it will often be neglected when we feel we must behave in certain ways to be good enough for others. Now we must tackle the challenge of the difference between intuition and living for others' opinions, and never let that paradigm determine your life. Your paradigm is the way you were consciously and unconsciously shaped by your environment during your childhood. The greater the distance between your paradigm and your inner truth, the worse you feel and the worse things will fall into place in your life.

When I coach people, I can intuitively find where in their lives their problems have arisen. It may be in their childhood or later in life, and in some cases even in past lives or blocks in their creation energy. I believe you can do the same derivation yourself, using your intuition. There is no rational thinking that consolidates this theory, even if quantum physics is approaching the area by leaps and bounds. But during my years as a coach, I have noticed that you get results that are out of the ordinary when using your intuition in this way.

Intuition is your soul contact with God, who gives you the ability to identify and solve negative energy blocks and thereby heal. I have come to the conclusion that this type of healing can happen in agreement with God when we have access to the original creation energy. It is a force far greater than what we intellectually can understand, where trust in God is sufficient for individual and collective healing. I am not talking about general belief in God or religion, but about that unconditional trust between you and God that can never be the same way between people. Sure, many of us rely on other people, but trust in God can be given without any doubt, because God is completely disconnected from all the ego's whims.

When no communication is present between the five levels of ourselves, we are not entirely balanced. Do you not have the life you want? Then find out what is not true. Where is the problem? Constantly seeking to rebalance ourselves heals us from the inside out.

Our internal imbalances are also reflected in our contact with the surrounding world, where imbalances are intercepted by others. The law of attraction, which frequently is mentioned in self-help books, says that what you have within you is reflected by others, be it positive or negative. It is not what you think or feel about yourself that determines what is reflected, but what you deep down in your soul perceive as the truth. Say you are thinking and feeling positive about yourself, but your soul paradigm says you are not good enough. Then it is this that you will attract, whether you like it or not. These soul traumas can be solved with the Soulbalance method, which makes the law of attraction meaningful and positive for everyone, even those with negative soul baggage.

Breaking the negative Paradigms

When you convert a negative paradigm to the life you want, you will face huge resistance. The hardest part of breaking negative habits—for example, alcoholism and anorexia—is not the physical aspects but the resistance to growth of your soul. But the more you do what is true for you, the more contact you get with your intuition. In the end, you will no longer do something based on the negative paradigms, because you know it will not lead you to where you want to be. Were you, for example, beaten as a child? You can be conditioned to keep and pass this pattern on to your children. But let yourself feel deep inside your soul whether this really is good for you and your children. Your intuition will guide you to the answer that abuse is not the solution, and your intuition will tell you that you need to find other ways to manage conflicts. You are now starting to live a life where you have full flow and do what is right for you and your children, regardless of what others think. Do you want a rich and challenging life? Then start now to do what feels right deep in your soul. Do things that might make you feel uncomfortable but that you know are right. Perhaps it is to make that phone call you are worried about, to talk to your child's teacher, or to get a new job. Follow your intuition and grow into the life you want to live and the person you want to be as long as you know its right for you, no matter how afraid you are. If you are encountering resistance in this process, you can solve these challenges with the Soulbalance method.

Chapter 3

The Soulbalance Method

It has taken me many years to develop the Soulbalance method to the level it has reached today. In the beginning, I solved the energy-related blockages with no structure, which went well when I helped others, but did not allow me to teach my clients to help themselves or, in turn, have the ability to help others. I then got intuitive messages from God how I should convey this information to you and others so you could heal yourself. The uniqueness of this method is that you solve your specific challenges yourself, or someone else helps you understand exactly what to solve. Each individual has a certain soul programming that consists of a mass of information about what we have experienced which is stored in the soul. All these memories are here to make us aware of what the soul needs to help us become the best we can be. Do you have a soul-related challenge? It will remind you until it has been noticed and resolved. When you use your intuition, which is God's gift to us, you can resolve exactly what the soul needs right now. It is like solving a soul puzzle where each piece has its unique significance for the whole. It is not until you create this intuitive contact with God that the real healing takes place. You can see it as a precision instrument in personal development. Once you acknowledge that you have wounds on a soul level, you have taken the first step toward self-healing.

The next step is to derive the underlying cause. When you find the underlying cause and its associated feeling or emotions, you start your real journey toward self-healing. No humiliation is too small to conquer. Actually, a single event from childhood is sufficient for agony. For the tens, hundreds or perhaps thousands of assaults, conscious or unconscious, that you have encountered, most without anyone deliberately wanting to harm you, the soul responds with pain and anxiety to give you the opportunity to realize where this pain originates. Had you not had pain on the outside, you would not be able to look inward and heal.

You can apply the Soulbalance method to any problem you feel you have. The core of each case is to find out what you want or should work with to heal in the best way. You can either choose something completely concrete, such as a stomachache, money trouble, or perhaps poor relationships. I use this way sometimes or search for a purely intuitive question. I then ask God what is important for me to work on for myself, or what my client needs help with in the case of a customer. Here it is important to release all thoughts and just dare to go into the intuitive soul level to get your response. Having identified your problem takes you back to the soul level, where you can use your intuition to look for the answer to when the underlying cause arose. Trust it! Then derive what happened and what feeling was locked in. You do not have to find the exact details, for the most important thing is to release the negative feeling.

An example of how to go about it: If you have a specific fear, write it down. Where on the soul level is this block? Here you can begin to derive the answer by setting up your intuitive communication with the universal soul. Ask and you shall get answers. Is the block in this life, past lives, or in the creation energy? The process may take a while before you feel comfortable with it. So it was even for me. In the beginning I asked questions all the time to the universal soul. Now I need only to ask two or three questions a day, because I gradually shifted from a rational way to an intuitive way of thinking. Everyone can do this. But then the question is: Why do all people not live in an intuitive way? The answer is that we are conditioned not to do so. Breaking your negative conditioning is probably the biggest challenge you will encounter in your life. All you need to do, and do now, is to make a decision, using your intuition, to train your intuition at all times from now on. By trusting your intuition, you will connect with the universal soul, who can guide you so that you can start living your inner truth. I am guided in everything I do, from coaching clients to writing this book. I no longer make decisions on a rational basis. But you must be prepared to go through all your fears to get to this point.

See your life as an imaginary timeline from your birth until today. See the timeline as a ruler with a variety of events that have occurred in life. On the line, you also have a variety of blocks which can, for example, be knowing that you're not good enough, believing that you never can make money, or knowing that you will never be completely well. When you begin to approach your blocks to change them, your paradigm says, "No, no, no!" Be aware that there are two types of fear. The first type you should listen to: "Do not jump off a bridge straight down into the asphalt." The second type of fear may prevent you from doing something that really is very positive for you, such as speaking in public or starting a family. When you really want to do something that develops you, but you are afraid, just do it in spite of how your paradigm reacts! The only thing that is important in such a situation is the derivation of where the fear comes from, so you can change your paradigm and make a lasting difference. However, if you just make an external change without having found the underlying cause of your negative paradigm, you do not solve your soul's message that brings you closer to your inner truth. You have not gotten the acceptance from your soul to find a new path. That is why mental training or psychotherapy is not sufficient enough to overcome problems in all instances—not if the problem sits deep in the soul.

How to heal yourself with the Soulbalance method

To help you get a better understanding of the relationship between the various levels which the Soulbalance method is based on, you can visualize their mutual relationship like this: When you see something physical, it has the relation 1 to 1. You can see and touch it, just as you can see and touch this book. You know that it exists.

When you think of something (mentally), it has the relation 1 to 9. You can not touch the idea but you can understand what you're thinking. On the next level, you have the feelings (emotional level) that have a ratio of 1 to 27. The feeling is even a bit more abstract than the idea. It is possible to find for most people, but it's easier to ask someone what they think than what they feel. If we then move on to your intuition, which resides on your soul level, it has a ratio of 1 to 29,000 which means that it can not be found in the usual way. The only way to land on this level is to release all internal and external demands on how you should be and act. Then you suddenly connect with your intuition, and you can resolve your soul challenges with the Soulbalance method. When you face a challenge and want to find its derivation, you start by writing it down on a piece of paper. Say you want to address a challenge concerning your bad self-esteem. You write "low self-esteem." Write down everything from one to ten causes and identify how many you are intuitively drawn to. In this case, you might circle three things. That means you need to solve your challenges with poor self-esteem at three different places in the soul so that your soul gets what it needs at this occasion.

Let's go ahead and investigate when the trauma occurred. Through the years I have come to the conclusion that the blocks may have occurred during three different stages and that the intellect often does not have a clue about how this will be resolved. Draw a straight horizontal line, -six to eight inches long. Divide the line into three equal areas. On the far right, write "This Life"—for the challenges you have in this life. In the middle write "Past Lives," and to the left, write "Creation Energy." Once you've written this up, circle the one of these three areas you are intuitively drawn to. If you circle "This Life," then you need to find the age when the trauma occurred, what happened, and who was involved to be able to access the feelings you want to release. Make a list from zero to your present age to identify the age you are drawn to. Let us, in this example, say you found the age of fourteen years.

Now the intuition begins to bring up old memories, so write down directly what happened and who was involved. Do not control your thoughts, but let go of all thoughts and the answer will come to you. Then identify what feeling or feelings have been locked in the soul. During the derivation process, there is always some hesitation. When in doubt, listen to your intuition and circle with a pen the option you feel attracted to. Gradually, it becomes easier to apply the method, and your intuition will develop. Then you do not always need to go through all the stages of writing up and circling your answers, as your intuition leads you right away. With the Soulbalance method, you will be guided to what you need to solve. Accept the answers that come to you. Just when the stress memory is released, one can react in every possible way. Some cry, others react more subtly. It works regardless of reaction, and a strong reaction is not necessarily better.

You have now learned to solve the challenges in this life, but many of us also have challenges from past lives that can hurt us just as much or more. I have had many clients who have experienced abuse or something else negative in a previous life and show the same strong symptoms as if it had happened yesterday. But once a person loses the block in the soul, he or she can be free and live a life more in balance. Let us say that we find the next cause in a past life (although it might well be that all three causes are in this very life). What happened and who was involved in the incident? Sometimes it can be individuals who you know in this life that you have challenges with in past lives. Relax and let everything come to you. What is the feeling or feelings related to the occurrence? Write down the feeling or feelings that come to you intuitively. Release all thoughts about what *ought* to surface and accept what comes instead. Now you have solved the cause of a challenge in a past life, and God will help you heal these negative memories that you carry in your soul. The third and final block is, in this case, a block in your creation energy. The energy block in your system is not connected to any individual, but here we are looking for often severe, general frustration and anxiety. This is not because the creation energy is negative, but because of the enormous power that was necessary to create everything. What feelings come to the surface when you solve this block?

You have already begun to make use of Soulbalance method, based on using your intuition and scanning your soul data bank in order to find your blocks and heal them with God's healing energy. You can use the Soulbalance method to identify problems, shortcomings, and negative paradigms that you have within yourself. Instead of consulting the various religions with your questions, you can now ask God through the universal soul, directly. Ask, and you will get answers. Ask what level your problem is and you will get answers. You might ask what you want at any time. You will never be judged and will always get accurate answers. In the beginning it may feel strange, but practice improves your skills. Do not be critical of yourself; focus on having faith in the process.

Now we come to the book's first exercise. Do not intellectualize when you do the exercises; strive to work intuitively, without censoring and limiting yourself. Do not judge what you come up with, just let it come. See the exercise as a basis for creating what you really want to have. The exercises in the book are overall very direct for you to work with your intuition as much as possible. You should be working more with intuitive decisions than having to create an intellectual understanding so that you do not fall into old, habitual thoughts, emotions, and behavior patterns. Dare to trust what you find in yourself. Do not think, but feel intuitively.

EXERCISE 3.1: *Find your blockages on the soul level*
This first exercise is to improve your self-image. The exercise is in this case related to this life. If you do not have a challenge with question number one below, then select the challenge you are struggling most with, and do the exercise the same way. It is more an example of how to use the method than how to tackle this particular issue. You can apply this exercise for any issue, at any time, and your intuition will be able to guide you to what you need.

The aim is to learn how to find your energy blocks and dissolve them on the soul level. Once the cause is resolved there, you can get a positive change even on the emotional, mental, and physical levels. That is what enables the Soulbalance method to help you get rid of problems where other methods fail. You will usually need to access the soul cause, and that is exactly what we do by working intuitively with this exercise.

1. Ask yourself if it is true that your parents never told you that they loved you. If so, you have a challenge with this issue; otherwise, you do not. If the issue is not relevant to you right now, then select another one that suits you.

2. Write a column of numbers from zero to your current age and let your finger be guided by your intuition and see where it ends. Circle the answer.

3. Let's say it lands on when you were four years old. What happened then? It may, for example, be a memory of your exposure to an unpleasant experience. If it is difficult for you to get a picture or feeling, write down a couple of things that happened when you were four years old. Circle the event that you are intuitively drawn to.

4. What people are involved in the incident and what is their part in what happened? Write down what comes to you.

5. What feeling or feelings does this provoke within you? Let's say that for you, it is the feeling of not being good enough.

6. Now you have found the cause intuitively, and you feel it is right. When you feel it is right, you can begin to heal with the help of God.

7. In the long run, the healing is also going to create new positive thoughts, feelings, and improved physical performance due to the soul cause being resolved.

8. If there are several basic causes of the external symptom, repeat the exercise until you intuitively feel that you have resolved everything that should be resolved right now.

Dare to be true to yourself at all times

We humans are all part of the same energy. That means that if you have a well-developed intuition, you can intuitively sense what is going on within and around you. Many sensitive people feel the energies of others. Be aware of this sensitivity and learn to filter negative energy and just let the energy you need reach your divine soul. Do not let negative energies like fear and hatred be a part of your life. This is easier said than done and requires both attention and training to develop your intuition to be able to make the right choices. When you develop and heal yourself, it is like cutting a diamond. It takes a tremendous force to cut a sparkling diamond to its true potential. When you encounter resistance and use the Soulbalance method, you will grow much faster than if you had not encountered any resistance at all. Therefore do not compare your challenges with others, because each individual encounters the challenge that suits him or her. It may seem unfair if someone achieves something very easy, but neither you nor I know what lies beneath the surface. A mistake that many make is just that, to compare their weaknesses with others' strength. But we need to solve our own challenges, regardless of how others are doing and how they see your challenges. Your development and your success are yours and yours alone to achieve, so do not be influenced by others' deficiencies and opinions about what is best for you. In God's eyes we all have equal value, so any kind of comparison with others is both unnecessary and energy consuming.

If you go through all the exercises in the book and find the derivation of various problems but cannot find the soul reasons to the problems, it might be because the issue is located in a former life, or in an energy block located in the creation energy. For many this may seem a little scary. But if you have challenges there and never have learned to look so far back, you could easily go the rest of your life seeking for something that you do not understand and do not know where to find. What you need to know is that some of us have had past lives and now have come back in this life to resolve what was not resolved on a soul level. When you find a block in a past life, you often recognize the feeling that comes to the surface, because you have become conscious of it through your intuitive derivation. Many of us have hundreds, sometimes thousands, of major challenges from past lives. When my clients began to be consciously aware of these blockages, they began to achieve results beyond the ordinary.

I ask you readers to take this to heart and really try to understand how it works. I was skeptical myself about past lives and whether God existed. Through my own and my clients' experiences of what happens in the coaching sessions, I have come to this conclusion: as long as this method achieves the wonderful things we have seen, I let go of the critique and surrender to my faith in the divine inside and outside myself. The most amazing healing often occurs in connection with letting go of the need for external proof that God really exists. In that moment the connection is reinforced. For some the challenges originate as far back as in the creation energy, where everything was created from one energy cell, which in its turn was created by God. Since we all have connection to the origin, we are all part of God, whatever we want to believe. Believing in yourself is the same as believing in God, because the power comes from the same origin. Some individuals are then challenged with blockages in the creation energy, where existential issues such as severe anxiety attacks often originate. Through also deriving the challenges to this dimension, many get rid of this long-standing struggle and feel truer in their lives.

The challenges are experienced by most people in this life, but if you do not the find solutions here, do not be afraid to look for energy blocks and paradigms created in past lives and the creation energy.

EXERCISE 3.2: *Not here and now, but just as important*
The exercise which now follows will help you find exactly where your blocks originate. We have practiced to find them in this life, but now you will also get a chance to see if you have blockages in past lives or in the creation energy. Often we have a symptom we carry on, but we cannot find a cause of the problem. It's not that the cause is not there; we just do not know where to look. In this exercise, you can get access to tools to resolve soul causes that you may not have been aware of in the past. You simply get an opportunity to find causes to blockages that you previously could not recognize, understand, or heal. Trust the answers you get through your intuition. Your intuition knows what right and wrong.

1. Draw a straight horizontal line where you write "This Life" at the far right on the line, "Past Lives" in the middle, and "Creation Energy" to the left. This line is like a timeline ranging from your original energy

creation to your life here and now. Now circle in which category of this life, past lives, or creation energy that your symptom originates.

2. Feel intuitively about the age in this life, or in which past life, your blockage occurred. For blockages in the creation energy, this needs not to be done, because the challenge there is not time related.

3. Find out what happened with help of the Soulbalance method. Do you have difficulty finding the precise cause? Write down three or four options and circle the one that feels intuitively right. You have now found the soul cause of the current challenge.

4. Are there any persons involved in the incident? Who are they, and what is their part of the whole? (This question does not apply to issues caused in the creation energy.)

5. Write down the feeling or the feelings that are part of the blockage. When you identify these to yourself, God will step in and help you heal the negative emotional memory of the soul.

6. Repeat steps one to five if necessary.

The soul perceives past lives as here and now. Have you been abused, or been the victim for something from a past life? This can give your body and energy system the external symptoms as if it happened yesterday. This explains why so many people do not get the help they need from traditional Western medicine. Conventional medicine often misunderstands and mistreats your external symptoms when there is an inner cause on the soul level. Often individuals treated with anxiety-reducing medicine put a lid on their creativity, instead of understanding that the patient may solve the real soul cause of his or her challenges. Many are sick, misunderstood, and excluded from society when the symptoms rather easily could be corrected with the Soulbalance method. In these cases, the conventional health care system does not have the wisdom to take care of these individuals and their soul-related problems. Conventional health care is absolutely nothing to belittle, but it is only useful for symptoms that are directly and solely related to the physical level. All conditions with phobias, fears, allergies, etc. that were linked to past life issues that my clients have freed themselves from had never been able to heal with a classical, scientific approach. Science would certainly like to have scientific proof of this, but every individual's unique happiness and balance will not be detected in a clinical study. God has made sure of this, as the biggest and best gifts in life, like happiness, love, faith, and trust, cannot be proven. The only proof I needed was that actual healing occurred individually and differently for each individual. Happiness often comes when you dare to let go and dare to create faith and confidence in yourself and God, who is free from all scientific standards and rules. Science has, of course, its proper place, but it is not the right tool to measure happiness.

If you have an external symptom that is not linked to the here and now, it goes without saying that it can be healed. Remember that healing is often more an insight that then leads to balance, and not something short term such as a painkiller, which just treats external symptoms and provides temporary relief. If you detect the soul cause and get both the emotional and soul understanding for what happened, you can heal on the soul level. This means that our external symptoms are signs for what we need to be aware of. In addition to classic symptoms for diseases, emotional expressions can sometimes be external symptoms of internal imbalances. External anger is always a sign of internal frustration. Find out what is this frustrating. What internal conflicts do you have that would aggravate you to feel such anger? What do you need to do to solve them? Derive the soul cause. Then change your behavior so it suits your true self. Self-contempt is sometimes related to the childhood you have had or think that you have experienced. Allergies are often symptoms of suppressed anger from one to six generations back. They are passed on from generation to generation and become stronger and stronger. Financial problems may be a lack of ability to understand one's self-worth. They can also go from generation to generation. Poor relationships are often a lack of respect and love for oneself. If you love yourself, you will select the relationship you want. When you heal yourself and get more self-respect, the relationship will reflect the inner feeling you have. The inner feeling reflects the exterior to create balance.

Soul Pain

The soul pain that many of us know is often just as devastating as or worse than the physical pain we could encounter by an accident. The physical pain is fully accepted by society, and you get all the help you need to heal it. The pain on the soul level is often invisible, ignored, and looked down on, but the pain is just as true as physical pain. It shows in the devastating effects soul pain has, often causing a destructive lifestyle with symptoms like anorexia, alcoholism, and in some cases even suicide. The more you have been violated in this life or past lives, the greater the risk that you will harm yourself and possibly others in this life. So many of us have, on one or more occasions, been violated one way or another. This can mean anything from actions that seem innocent, such as being forced to sit alone during lunch at school, to traumas such as being beaten or raped. All these violations affect us whether we like it or not. Depending on how sensitive we are, the violations affect us in different ways, which does not make us weaker, but more responsive to external humiliation.

Often it is the individuals with much to offer in relation to their internal truth that face difficulties. The reason for this is that those who have much to give often stand for ideas and opportunities that their paradigm or others do not recognize, so when they try to live their truth, a mountain of resistance is created by the paradigm. Often the resistance of the paradigm is so large that they do not dare to face their fears and live their truth. They start to falter, their truth is ruined by the violations, and they start to live a life in which they harm themselves, and in some cases others, because they feel that they never can realize their inner truth. Without hope, the individual stops caring and lands in some type of desperation. When this does happen, the soul truth gets more and more turned off and then is completely alien to the individual. If the ethical framework which we all have naturally in us is turned off, then there is no inner ethical framework anymore and disaster strikes. I have seen that all healthy individuals have an ethical framework which allows them to distinguish between right and wrong. It has nothing to do with the laws, but a soul in balance that is free from negative conditioning knows what is right and wrong with its unique way of communicating with the universal soul, where all truths are present. But because of the resistance of the paradigm, which in some cases is very extreme, this inner ethical system can fail. Thank God there is hope even for those who have these types of challenges.

The problem is, unfortunately, that the most aggrieved individuals have lost their ability to show that they are doing wrong. If we do not know that we have made a mistake, then what should one seek help for? What is unique about the Soulbalance method is that we can circumvent the whole paradigm which puts an end to the positive thoughts and feelings that we really are entitled to. By deriving and solving the soul-level blockages, individuals can begin to heal from the inside out and begin to establish an inner soul dialogue where they know they are good enough. Eventually the insight not to harm others will occur. With these insights even the most vulnerable and damaged can heal. The key is to reclaim the soul-level insight that we always are good enough. If I feel that I am good enough, I will not harm myself or others.

EXERCISE 3.3: *To dissolve blockages in the intuitive and healing flow*
Sometimes you can have a blockage in the flow between the five levels, between the physical, mental, emotional, soul, and spiritual level, in the said order. This then stops your intuitive ability to ask God how you should solve your blockages. You can also have a stop in the flow in the opposite direction, so that the healing ability of God is blocked or restricted. These two blocks are not there to stop you, but to make you

aware of how to resolve your life issues. The purpose of the following exercise is to show that there is always a possibility for you to maintain your intuition and your healing ability. The exercise describes what you need to do when your faith in God and yourself is lacking. Of course, everyone wants to feel the healing and intuitive power all the time, but self-doubt, attacks from others, or any other challenge can put your trust, and therefore your relationship with God, on temporary hold. You can always go back to this exercise if you ever feel that the intuitive response is lacking. It's like a soul service for your divine flow.

1. Find out if you have any blockage in the intuitive flow by intuitively identifying a "yes" or "no" answer on paper, and circle the answer that you get.

2. Do you find that you are blocked? Where is the blockage: in this life, in past lives, or in the creation energy? Circle what you intuitively are attracted to.

3. Look intuitively at what age in this life, or in which past life, your blockage occurred. At the creation energy level, you do not need to find a certain time frame, because the challenge there is not time related.

4. Find out what happened with the Soulbalance method. Do you have difficulty with finding the precise issue? Write down three or four options and circle the one that feels right. You have now found the soul cause of the current challenge.

5. Are there any persons involved in the incident? Who are they and what is their part of the whole issue? (This question does not apply to the creation energy.)

6. Write down the feeling or the feelings that are part of the blockage. When they surface from your subconscious mind, God will step up and help you heal the negative emotional memory of the soul.

7. Follow the same process for the healing flow in the other direction (steps -one through six). You are now on track to create the flow and the intuition you want in your life.

8. Repeat the exercise if necessary.

What makes the Soulbalance method work so well? What is unique is that the method helps you bypass your rational thoughts and feelings when you solve an issue in your life. Deep in the soul you have all the answers about what is right for you, but it is not always simple to dare to trust your intuition. Actually we should do it, but because we often are full of negative conditioned thoughts and feelings from this life and sometimes past lives, it is not always possible. Often, the mental and emotional blocks are so strong that you cannot use reason to resolve your internal challenges. That is one reason why so many creative people through the centuries have used drugs in order to circumvent the conditioned thought and feelings defense. Many great things have been created under that influence, for example, by actors and musicians. But there is a serious setback with this approach. It never gives you the insights you need to move on in life. You become dependent on a substance of some kind to be able to create. If you, however, learn how to derive things directly from your soul level, you also get the soul level insight you need to take you to the next level and the next and so on. You have now created healing on the soul level that will help you move forward at all times in life.

I want to describe a case involving a client who took drugs to solve his everyday problems and help the creative process. The person was sent to me by his parents because they did not think that their son behaved and functioned normally in life. The boy was eighteen years old and was perceived by his parents as generally lethargic and uninterested in everything. The boy met me initially against his will, because who wants to be told what to do? I explained that our meetings had nothing to do with a reporting requirement to the parents, but that I could help him entirely independently of them. Then suddenly he opened up entirely, and he briefed me on how his life really was. The boy had a severe drug addiction, not because of his friends, but because he felt so unwelcome and questioned by his parents. We worked with these challenges using the Soulbalance method, and tremendous healing of the boy took place. Within a few weeks he went from drug dependency to being a free, creative soul who began creating the life he wanted, not the life his parents wanted him to live. Today he lives according to his inner truth, which previously his conditioning thought was impossible. The drugs were only one way for the boy to get through the days full of anxiety and disappointment in life. If he had fought his conditioning in a traditional way and just tried to stop taking the drugs, no permanent change would have occurred. Here it was necessary to use the Soulbalance method to heal the boy's self-loathing, which he felt in association with his parents, so that a positive, long-term solution could be achieved.

Ready to start the Dialogue?

Now you have the choice to become your own spiritual decision maker. By having more and more contact with your soul truth, you will also receive and retrieve more information from God on the spiritual level. The spiritual level has a lot of exciting things to offer. All negatives can there be transformed and turned into opportunities. You will not stop having challenges, but you will see them in a completely different way. Life suddenly will feel meaningful instead of meaningless as otherwise is common if you do not have contact with the spiritual level. The spiritual level is like fuel for your soul engine, which loads and fills your system with energy as long as you are true to yourself. You do not have to be true against someone else to get this contact. This is a dialogue between you and God that can lead exactly where you want. Everything great that has been created on this earth was created by faith. God's faith first created nature, animals, and human beings. Then God has worked through us to create what man can create, and that process also needs faith. Divine faith does not have to do with going to church or other religious phenomena, but it could just as easily be about a businessman or woman who brings humanity to greatness through his or her faith, which may seem very superficial and nonspiritual to others. But indirectly, it is always God's power behind all creation. This does not diminish our human ability, but without God our creative ability would not be possible. God does not try to steer us to show his strength, but

God is always with us, whether we like it or not. So why run away from something that exists? We can not change seasons, the sun and the moon are always there, and we do not deny their presence, but we often deny God's presence as if it were something strange. Do you really think that nature could create something as advanced as all life on earth without a higher intelligence, this intelligence being God? See faith as an opportunity to take advantage of the huge divine power waiting for you, which can give you an added dimension in life and create a larger sense, free from the ego's desire. What you then do with this power is up to you.

Chapter 4

Your inner Truth

How do you find the right path in life? How do you find your inner truth? You are living your inner truth when you can do what you really want with your life, when you have the opportunity to exploit your full potential. Your inner truth has nothing to do with what others want for you. It has nothing to do with what your paradigm says, but it is completely focused on what you, deep inside, know that you are destined to do. We have all been given various unique gifts with which we can enrich ourselves and the world. By using these gifts, we enrich ourselves and others with the nourishment which we are destined to receive and give. Once you start living your inner truth, you automatically begin to heal. One part of the self-healing is that you live according to your inner truth and the second part is that you free yourself from what is preventing you from getting there, through freeing yourself from negative blockages and their negative symptoms. It is not enough just to do what feels right in your life, living your inner truth. Traditional coaching works most often with helping you to set a goal and then offer you the tools to get there. But this active change in the direction of your inner truth will only work if your soul is free from blockages and willing to do the change. An inner truth involving, for example, material success is impossible to achieve without first ensuring that the soul is free from the negative conditioning that prevents the inner truth from being realized. Similarly, it is useless to solve the conditioning on the soul level if no connection is made to do an external change in the direction of living one's inner truth. To solve all of one's greatest fears and phobias without daring to take the step and challenge them in daily life is not the way to become whole.

Say you have solved a social phobia with the Soulbalance method. Then, it is natural to challenge it and see if you need to do something that will change your old negative thought and behavior patterns so that you also have a lasting, positive change in the external behavior. It is precisely this interaction to solve blockages with the Soulbalance method and to live one's inner truth that is the key to success for virtually everyone I encounter. Only then is the soul ready for the insights and the motivation it needs to help us create the success we really want. Sometimes it does not go as expected immediately, but it is not because the inner truth is wrong; mostly it is because of the negative paradigms which still lie locked in the soul. Go back and release them with the Soulbalance method so that you take one step closer to the life you want.

How do you connect with your inner truth?

1. Live your life fully. Think through what you want with your life and how you want to live it to really give it a chance. Stop living your life to be good enough in someone else's eyes.

2. Think about what you want to achieve. What do you really want to do for yourself and others? What would you do with your life if you did not have any limitations?

3. Transform your limitations into opportunities. Write down the limitations you believe you have both inside and outside of yourself. Derive and dissolve the limitations with the Soulbalance method. Repeat until you feel that you are free from what is limiting yourself.

4. Set measurable goals for what you would like to achieve within a year. Describe them in detail.

5. Create action. What do you need to do to achieve these goals? Write an action plan to help you act your way to success.

Imagine that you wake up in the morning full of confidence for what life has to offer. You have big plans for life, with various activities that makes you grow as a person, while you can treat yourself to the lifestyle you want. Now imagine that you wake up every morning, disappointed in yourself and in others because of where life has taken you. Everything seems impossible, and today's activities barely get done, only to keep you alive. Which of these two scenarios would you choose? Of course most people would choose scenario number one, where life is full of opportunities, but for some reason, more and more of us are living according to scenario number two. Why is this so?

Many people come to me who want to have balance in life. The first thing I ask is: Where are you in your life? The answer is often not the same as where they want to be in life. There can be different answers in the areas of health, finances, and relationships. These are the three main areas that most often are discussed. Sometimes it's just an imbalance in one of these areas, sometimes the problem is just one specific issue, but there often two or all three areas are involved in a person's imbalance. Some know where they want to be, and others do not. But your inner truth, which is the soul's clear, intuitive answer, knows what is best for you, guaranteed. How are you able to find your inner truth, unless you begin this process and seek what you really want and have the capacity to do? Your true capacity is perhaps not the capacity that you now think you have, for it can be limited, but your intuitive soul power can take you to where you really belong at all levels. To be true to yourself, you need to prioritize yourself and the activities that are right for you, before you try to live up to other people's expectations. When you are true to yourself, your soul gets the nutrition it needs to help you feel good, get good results, and be happy. The reason that the soul reacts so strongly when you go in what, for you, is a nontrue direction is not to be mean. Instead it wants to help you to see things in a way that helps you be true to yourself in life, the life you know deep inside that you want to live. The more you deny your inner truth and put your intuitive gift on hold, the more signals you will get from yourself and your surroundings that you are on the wrong track.

In the beginning it may be subtle things, such as your conscience bothering you or having difficulty sleeping. But if you do not listen to your inner truth, you will eventually get very strong signals in the form of financial troubles, bad health, poor relationships, or anything else. At the same time, when you start living your inner truth, you will encounter resistance. The more you start living your inner truth, the greater resistance you will encounter. That is because your paradigm has strong resistance and wants you to you remain in old habits. It may feel like going through purgatory as unpleasant feelings from your subconscious that limit you will surface. You need to identify the blockages that create this resistance. What are you afraid of when you create the life you want? Write down what you feel intuitively, derive the reasons, and then find the soul cause with the Soulbalance method. Is it unconscious blockages? They will limit you on your way to your inner truth without you knowing it. What you are not aware of is often the most difficult to resolve. Negative external results always have a reason, and if you do not know what it is, it is a subconscious blockage. By using your intuition, you will also be able to solve these challenges, although it may require some training.

What do you now need to do to live your inner truth? What should you do not to live your negative paradigm over and over again?

1. Find your inner truth. Do what suits you, and not what you think you should do to be accepted by others. Many perceive this as selfish, but if we could all do what we are meant to do, we would have a greater balance in society than we have today. Imagine living your life fully, and dare to take on all the challenges to make the trip.

2. Do not let others decide your inner truth; only you know what it is. Many will have opinions when you start doing things that benefit your life. Choose to live your life fully, free from others' standards and desires. It is not your obligation to live according to others' limitations.

3. Do you want good relations and cooperation with others? Ensure that all involved may be one with their inner truth. If we are who we want to be, and our loved ones are who they want to be, we automatically create relationships in balance. The same is true in all collaborations. Do you feel that a relationship is not working and that you cannot accept each other's truths? If so, it can certainly be worthwhile to look around for new friends and relationships.

4. Never go against your inner truth. No money in the world is worth it. When you are on the road to your inner truth, the obstacles will accumulate. There may be internal obstacles, with paradigms which say that you are not good enough or worthy of success. As soon as you start to create what you want, the negative energy will remind you of its presence to tell you that it is not willing to let go of you voluntarily.

5. It can also be external obstacles that show their presence. When you leave the old conditioning behind and evolve, it can be unfamiliar and uncomfortable for those surrounding you, because they have to adapt to your changes. It is often because they are stuck but see you realizing yourself, which can raise strong emotions within them. Many may then try to stop your progress, sometimes consciously, but often unconsciously, because they are conditioned to respond in that way.

Actually the whole idea in society that we are not allowed to have success is one great individual and collective paradigm that prevents us from realizing our dreams. Here you need to trust your intuition and go the way you want regardless of the resistance you meet. If you dare to go your intuitive way, the resistance will disappear when it cannot affect you any more. You are now growing through your challenges and creating the life you want. Never let yourself be tempted by short-term success based on the ego's will, for in the long run it leads to long-term adversity. Life is for us to grow and use courage to challenge ourselves to become the best we can be. When we have no reason to grow, the striving to live fully ceases. Many are dead long before their bodies leave this world. Often our conditioning from generations back has destroyed all faith in possibilities and happiness. This can change, and it is simple, but not easy: the idea for self-fulfilment and understanding one's constraints is simple, but once you do change, you will meet resistance. You will certainly encounter all sorts of fears and challenges when you take the step and dare to become the best you can be. The only way to achieve balance and happiness is just to start working on the internal and external changes. Later in this chapter you will find exercises to help you get started with this work.

Fears

Do you have something you are really afraid of, but which is harmless and would give you a strong sense of success and happiness if you mastered it? It is these fears that you need to challenge to get the balance and the success you want, but perhaps have not already achieved. These fears sit as brakes on your way to balance, not only in the area that the fear is about, but also in all other areas in which you want to achieve success. Say you have a fear of speaking in public. You avoid making speeches because it is such an unpleasant feeling when you stand there. The problem is that this fear also locks your success in other areas, like alcohol problems that often causes trouble in several areas, such as finances, health, and relationships. The fear of speaking in public is like alcohol problems—an external symptom of something much larger and more extensive. If you only attack the symptom, you can at best make a behavioral change where you can manage to stand in front of others or be a sober alcoholic. But it is not until you find the real cause, which can be anything from low self-esteem to depression, that you really can solve your challenge for good. The basic reason that you do not dare speak in front of people can influence you directly, so that you do not dare to give lectures on your favorite subject, but what is worse is that it affects you negatively in other areas as well. The soul cause—say, in this case, poor self-esteem—attracts everything to reinforce your bad self-esteem. Once you have dissolved the internal cause, you will also have positive outcome concerning other areas in life because the soul cause is related to so much more than just the symptoms that you just solved.

EXERCISE 4.1: *Release yourself from your fears*

1. Identify the fear. What are you afraid of? If you do not know, then it is difficult to conquer. Become your own expert to find what your fear is. Some say that they are not afraid of anything, but their limited external performance shows something completely different. Fear can then be so suppressed in the subconscious mind that you have to look for external symptoms instead of an inner fear. In this case it might be money trouble that is the issue.

2. Derive, with help of the Soulbalance method, whether the fear comes from this life, a past life, or from the creation energy.

3. If the fear has its origin in this life, find the age when it was created. For the other two options, it is sufficient enough to find out what happened. Do this step even if the fear originated in this life.

4. Are there any people involved in what happened? What is their function in the whole thing? This step does not apply to the creation energy.

5. What feeling or feelings will now rise to the surface? Experience them. Let them be a part of you. Once you can accept the feeling or feelings, they are ready to leave you. They have done their work, and you have solved this by finding their cause. You cannot avoid the unpleasant feelings in the long run if you want to be free. To meet them and detach yourself from their negative force and effect is the only solution.

6. God will now help you to get rid of these feelings' negative impact on you.

Trust

Confidence that everything will be all right is perhaps the most crucial but most underestimated tool in order to really achieve the success and balance you want. You can try to push for the results only on a physical level, but it does not work long term. You can add your power of thought to produce results. You can become emotionally involved with your project. But it is not until you realize you have everything you need that the pieces really fall into place. How do you then get this insight? It can be so different for everyone and is highly individual. In my case, my trust was developed primarily for three reasons:

1. I started using the Soulbalance method, which I did not at first quite understand, but which did so much for me and for others. I then realized that the healing I and others received did not come from any human but from God. Just imagine there is such a force. It was great and gave me the trust I needed.

2. I really began to see the miracles that the Soulbalance method could do. The internal gratitude I felt when I solved all of my approximately twenty allergies was huge, and when my clients also confirmed similar stories, my trust in the divine began to grow even more.

3. My trust in God has saved my life on several occasions, as when the invisible hand takes hold of and prevents one from crossing the street in a situation that could have been serious. I have seen so many natural and supernatural things happen that I have come to the conclusion that in the end it is still not me who decides about everything, but I follow the divine flow with trust and look where it will take me.

For you the trust will perhaps be created in a completely different way. The important thing is that you finally know that you are good enough and know that there is a greater force, God, that confirms this, no matter what your paradigm or others say or think. You have now, hopefully, the internal trust in the soul, and you know that the day will come when you reach your goals and get the balance you seek. When you have faith in the divinity within yourself and at large, you cannot lose regardless of external circumstances. When you have trust in difficult, trying times, you develop another dimension of consciousness and inner wisdom. This internal understanding of the importance of trust leads you to success. The key is to have trust in all situations, even when you are tested to the breaking point. Otherwise, you can easily be trapped in anxiety and fear regardless of external circumstances. This applies to many who are successful only on the exterior. They have all the money in the world, but they are still stuck in fear and apprehension. Without the internal trust, their money only strengthens their fears and concerns.

Always trust your own ability. It does not pay off to ask someone to make your decisions, because it is an indication of your lack of faith in yourself. When you are in crisis, it is only your inner trust that helps you. To trust one's own ability is extremely undervalued. Actually, it the key to making everything else work in your life. Without trust in yourself, the trust in God will also falter, because your trust in yourself is the key to daring to trust God. Rely on God. What is God to you, and what does he or she mean to you? Take time to really examine your relationship with God. Have you been conditioned by the view that God does not exist? You will perhaps conclude that this picture is not your actual truth. What do you now have to lose by trusting that divine power? For my own part, I was very skeptical about everything that had to do with God and religion. But I was feeling so terribly bad. I gave my faith a chance because I had nothing to lose. Behind my atheistic childhood there were a multitude of religious ideas and attitudes hidden. I discovered, among other things, that I was afraid that I was not good enough for God and that I, at the same time, was extremely disappointed and angry at God. If God existed, then why was my life and many others' lives a living hell? What I then discovered was that God was there for me, not to please me, but to help me be true to myself and help me to develop. With this insight, I could go on and accept what came to me in a completely different way than before.

Intuition

There are two ways to arrive at a decision in every situation. One is the rational, which we have learned from the environment since childhood, while the other one is to make intuitive decisions that are linked to you as an individual, regardless of what or who has conditioned you. Each individual has in his soul the intuitive ability to create what is really right for him or her. As a child you always had access to this intuitive force until others transmitted their views, thoughts, and feelings to you. The paradigm may have ruined your life, but you always have a choice between using the intuitive power and not doing so. You can at any time decide not to let your paradigm control you anymore. The decision means that now you have taken a first step towards your true self. But to get there, you need to re-create your intuitive ability, which always been there but remained well hidden under all layers of conditioning. It can be a strenuous and demanding task, since intuition needs to be trained and challenged to reach full capacity. But it is well worth the effort, and I would not give away my intuition for all the money in the world. Not that money is unimportant to me, but because I put an even larger value on the gift we have received from God.

Consider now where your conditioning has taken you and where your intuition would like to take you. Which scenario seems most appealing? Let's say you have had a life filled with challenges ranging from poverty to negative thoughts and emotions that affect your health and your relationships. This is not really you, but the conditioning you have gotten from your surroundings. Depending on your paradigm, it looks like you often create thoughts, feelings, and even physical results that you do not want.

Do you want to get rid of this and create the life that you really long for deep inside? The key, then, is to learn how to use your intuition, which is your contact with your soul and also your contact with God. Once you make intuitive decisions, your life will be the way you really want, regardless of circumstances. Your intuition is your key to balance and success.

Follow your intuition:

• You have a choice between the intuitive and the rational decision, at all times. Where has the rational choice taken you until now?

• Choose what feels right for you deep inside and do not let others affect you. Unfortunately many of us allow others to determine our lives. Do you really want your neighbors' or your parent's opinion to decide what you should do with your life?

• Do not look at past performance when making a decision, because it is then that your paradigm is speaking. You can now decide for yourself to create success on the soul level. It can then take some time before what you manifest reaches the physical level. But keep with you the insight that it will happen. When you do an intuitive and healing change on the soul level, the energy blockage for the current challenge is resolved. Then it takes some time before you see your intuitive decision become physical reality. Have faith that it will happen. Often we let our conditioning come in and disrupt this process, and then God's healing function cannot do what it is supposed to do.

• If you are afraid, but what you face feels right deep inside, just carry on. Fear is just in your conditioning, which you must learn to overcome to reach your inner truth.

• Dare to trust your intuition on all occasions. If you want divine results, then there is really no other way to go. You may have carried on negative thoughts or had negative results as long as you can remember. Once you begin to create success and balance with your intuition, your paradigm will not be valid anymore, and you can now truly create what you want. You may get new thought patterns, experience new positive feelings, and, when the negatives show up, you understand them much better and can handle them and see them as part of your development towards a freer soul and a happier life.

Exercises to help you find your inner Truth

EXERCISE 4.2: *Your inner truth*

We have often learned since childhood to be honest and true to others, but when have you been really true to yourself lately? The purpose of the following exercise is to find your inner truth so that you can take yourself from where you are to where you want to be.

1. Draw a dot at the left side on a piece of paper. The dot illustrates the time when you were born. Draw a horizontal line to the right from the dot so that the right point indicates where you are today. You have reached this point thanks to/because of your conditioning from the environment. Now draw a line diagonally up to the right from your birth dot, so that it forms an upward skiing slope. The difference between the two right points is the difference between your inner truth and your conditioned life. It is this difference that makes you feel out of balance, out of place at work, and short of money. All these symptoms are the soul's way of saying "change direction" until you live in a way consistent with your inner truth.

2. What do you now need to do to move from where you are to where you want to be? What do you need to develop, change? Write a list of at least ten things involving an active change.

3. Establish an action plan, and plan when to make the changes. Our conditioning has a tendency to postpone everything to the future, so give

precise dates for when things should be done—for example, that you should lose ten pounds by a certain date.

4. Act now, step by step, to free yourself from your old paradigm. It can be impossible to see five pounds of weight loss in your mind, but scheduling an hour-long walk five days a week and eating healthier will take you there. It is like building a house from scratch. Make sure to place each stone securely, seeing the finished house in front of you as goal. Do not worry if it will happen or not, but just make up your mind to make it happen.

5. You can solve the limiting paradigm you meet along the way using the Soulbalance method. Repeat step five, if necessary, until the paradigms cannot affect you negatively anymore.

Do not despair if it seems too demanding. Maybe you start by trying to change one or two things. That is fine. The important thing is that you actively start to make the change that you need to make to break your old negative conditioning and habitual patterns. Do not be too hard on yourself, but do what feels right for you right now. When you get in touch with your inner truth, you know you are on the right path. Everything is not easy all the time, but you will get a flow with what you do and you will feel good. You can only achieve that by starting to use your intuition. Your conditioning can be so strong that you can only change your life by training yourself to listen to your intuition. Your parents, your neighbors, your friends might say that it is not possible, but does your intuition say that? You can choose. That way it will work.

EXERCISE 4.3: *Be convinced that your inner truth really is right for you*

If you do not live your inner truth, you can feel bad. You can live your life so that it outwardly looks like you live as you want, but you still feel bad inside because you have not dissolved your internal blockages. You can also learn how your inner truth works, but you do not execute this in how you live. When you do not have balance both inside and externally, you will not feel complete balance in life. The feeling of imbalance exists for you to get the momentum to create change and live your inner truth.

1. Begin by asking yourself what makes you happy. What work do you want to do? Your intuition may say that you want to start a clothing company. You have found your inner truth about work. Of course, you can use this exercise in other areas that affect your inner truth.

2. Now you may still feel insecure and afraid. If so, search deeper. Write down the question: "Is it right for me to start a clothing company?" Write down *yes* and *no,* and circle the answer that you automatically are drawn to. Let's say you circle *yes,* you have this dream, but there is something in your past that makes you not dare to go for it. Ask yourself the question now: what it is that prevents you from reaching your inner truth? Use the Soulbalance method to identify the answer that comes to you.

3. Does the blockage come from this life, a past life, or from the creation energy? Circle the answer that you are drawn to.

4. If you circle *this life,* then you must come to a conclusion about when the incident forming the basis for your blockage occurred. Write down

the year the blockage occurred. Let your intuition guide you towards the right year. For past lives or blockage that has to do with the creation energy, you do not have to find out when the blockage occurred. You can do it if you want, but it is not necessary for the success of this exercise.

5. Then ask yourself, what happened? If you do not directly find the cause, continue on, write up a variety of events that could be the cause, and circle the one that intuitively feels right.

6. Are there any people involved? Write down who they are and their part in the whole blockage (this section does not apply to the blockages that are derived from the creation energy, as these blockages are not related to humans).

7. Once you find the event, you can find the derivation of the feeling or feelings that have been locked and that are now blocking you. Maybe it is the feeling that you could not succeed or that you did not feel loved.

8. Now intuitively feel whether your inner truth feels one hundred percent. If not, repeat the exercise until it feels right.

Once you start using your intuition, you will be confronted with the rational thinking, which may have dominated your life one hundred percent earlier. In the beginning, you may hesitate a bit about what is intuitively right for you. In my case, intuition creates joy and balance, while my rational thoughts take me back to the hopelessness and depression that I experienced when I followed my conditioned habits. Always be aware that there is the rational way to look at the conditions that are influenced by your parents, what you learned at school or read in the newspapers, and so on, and then there is the intuitive way. The rational way is a kind of conditioning that often controls us without us being aware of it. Distinguish the rational (paradigm) from the intuitive. Envision having two doors in front of you when you ask yourself what to do. One door opens for rational thinking, the other for the intuition.

If you choose the rational door and the rational responses, you will be good at living up to other people's standards. But the longer you live away from your inner truth, the worse you will feel. However, if you live in an intuitive manner, constantly aware of whether what you are doing is right for you or not, you will choose very different answers. When you begin your journey to your inner truth, you will constantly open new doors for each new choice you face. Each time, you can either choose the intuitive truth or the rational door. The more you choose the rational door, the more your paradigm controls you. The more you practice, the less inclined you are to choose the rational door and the rational responses, and the easier it becomes for you to choose the intuitive way. Most people make rational choices all the time, rather than using their intuition. The more you learn to listen to your intuition, the more rarely you need to ask the universal soul for answers. You will eventually get a clear, nice feeling inside you that tells you when you are right without having to ask the universal soul for answers. If you choose the wrong door in an isolated situation, it is perhaps not so detrimental, but long-term, repeated selections of the wrong doors, according to your negative conditioning, will eventually take you to a completely different place in life than where you want to be. Perhaps it will begin with a door, a choice, but it will end with a personal catastrophe as your inner truth is ignored too often.

It is important to emphasize that your intuition is a sensation that is not always consistent with what we usually call a gut feeling. The gut feeling may be a decision made according to your paradigm. Have you been conditioned in the wrong way? You will have a negative gut feeling even if you are facing something positive. Previously, I myself often felt in my stomach if something was right or wrong, but it was not my intuition that gave me the answers, but my conditioned gut feeling. In this way, I developed a variety of phobias and other negative habits, not because they were right according to my intuition and inner truth, but because they were what my paradigm told me was right for me. So the gut feeling is based on conditioned thoughts, feelings and behavior. Intuition, however, is the response to you from God and the universal soul, who has no preconceived ideas or demands on you. No paradigm governs the intuition, so it is therefore totally objective if it is used properly. How should we then know if we make decisions with our gut feeling or intuition? I usually describe the presence of the intuition as being guided to make decisions or to remove blockages or something else through an experience that is something more than ordinary thoughts and feelings. For me there is such a big difference between my thoughts and my intuition that I know when I come in contact with my intuition rather than my conditioned gut feeling. This text has nothing to do with my conditioned thoughts, for my conditioned mind is not able to achieve these insights and solutions. But my intuitive side that conveys God's message can do just that. The more you rely on your intuition, the faster and deeper healing you achieve. To love yourself, knowing that you are good enough, will be a natural part of your life. You are now no longer dependent on approval from others to feel good enough. Basically, you just know that you are good enough in yourself and that you are good for the whole (God). If any other person says that you are not good enough, it is their opinion, and as long as you do not take that as the truth, it can never harm you.

To act to Achieve your Goals

As you now use the Soulbalance method and feel more and more in balance, you get the strength to make the external changes that bring you closer to a life according to your inner truth. In this case an action plan is required. When you start creating an action plan, it must be synonymous with your inner truth. Ponder what you need to change to get your inner truth manifested in your life. Set up an action plan with a clear time frame. Divide the plan into subgoals which also have dates set when things should be done. Include health, relationships, and finances in your plan, and think of the whole picture. Break down the plan on a detailed level so that you can divide the week into days, and enter a number of things that must be done each day that are in line with your inner truth. Those who do this one hundred percent reach their inner truth and experience balance and success. All individuals have different opinions on how detailed the plan should be and how much to include. Basically you can divide people in three categories according to how they plan to reach their goals and feel good: 1) those that need to set low goals that they always reach with a wide margin; 2) those that require medium-high goals that they just barely reach; 3) those who need to set high goals and often do not reach them in full, but are happy and successful in what they actually achieve. There is a cultural aspect to this. Americans often set sky-high goals and like that approach. We Swedes are often a bit more cautious. But all categories are available in all countries and cultures. The ones that set the standard too high or low relative to what is optimal for them often feel unfulfilled. I need skyrocketing goals for good health, while my mom taught me to be careful in everything. That paradigm has caused much misery for me. So which type are you?

1. Should set low goals for good health

2. Should set medium-high goals to feel good

3. Should set high goals to feel good

Use and let your intuition guide you to the option that is right for you. Customize the plan according to your needs.

To act is often easier said than done. Most of us are specialists in postponing things and "doing it later." Most of us even have difficulty in breaking our habits. The power of habit is great and can often prevent us from reaching our inner truth. But when you start to solve the blockages, energy is released so that you get the power to change thought and behavior patterns. Be prepared, however, because your belief system can start to protest when you conquer your paradigm and break your habitual patterns. Accept the feelings that surface, no matter how uncomfortable they are. You develop, refine your intuition, and create new soul-level insights to change direction in life.

After using the Soulbalance method for a while, you will have trained your intuition to a level that it facilitates your daily work to come closer to your inner truth. The closer you get, the easier it gets. In the end, you will have broken your old paradigms and habitual patterns and will begin to live your life, not the life that someone else has decided that you shall live. Now, life is an exciting challenge to be the best you can be. While you are on the way to your goals and your internal truth according to the plan, you must be flexible enough to change them if necessary. We have the greatest creative ability when we can go from one project to another without feeling the internal pressure that it all has to be finished, not for the success but for the almost obsessive behavior that keeps our creativity in check. Warning signs are, for example, if one has to wash the car on a Sunday, clean up on a Monday, and shop on a Wednesday without leaving any room for spontaneous activities.

Eleven tips for increased flexibility:

1. See every day as a new beginning where you have every opportunity to develop and win. Remember that we all wake up to the same day and often the same opportunities.

2. Make sure you leave a little room for spontaneity in life. Consider all the times you did something spontaneously. Life's best moments often

occur thanks to spontaneity. Maybe it leads to a new job, a relationship, or a new business idea.

3. Do not try to be someone you're not, but instead be yourself at all times. Are you trying to put up a strong exterior but feeling very different inside? It costs more than it is worth.

4. Do not wait to change, but do it right now. Would you like to do something with your life? Do it today, for tomorrow one more day has further passed out of your life.

5. "What if things go wrong?" These are perhaps the worst words to say. "What if" changes nothing. Anything can go wrong at any time in life, so it makes no sense to focus on it. That does not mean that you should live life in a foolhardy way. Life must have more to give than the fear to live.

6. Transform "what if things go wrong" to "I believe it is possible" Those who see possibilities in everything sooner or later create opportunities, while pessimists will sooner or later have their negative fears confirmed.

7. Why be done with life when you can get so much more out of life? Many of us want to be finished with something so we can relax and maybe not work anymore. But to fulfill your dreams is precisely the driving force to create something new that keeps you young.

8. Remember that nothing is impossible until you decide that it is so. What type of life has your paradigm decided on for you? If you want

more out of life, but do not see any possibility to achieve it, then it is your conditioning talking to you.

9. What opportunity should you go for right now? Think of one thing right now that you want to change in your life. When will the change take place?

10. What is in the way to keep that change from being made already? The excuses we have are many and often poor. Stop blaming others when things do not turn out as you want.

11. Failure is a good start. We have been conditioned since childhood that it is awful to do something wrong. Here we ignore the large mistakes made by us or anyone else and concentrate on the small things where we make a mistake and think we are useless. You have taken a step closer to your inner truth by daring to try out new ideas, no matter how it goes.

Chapter 5

Let your Intuition Guide you

Are you stuck in old, negative habit patterns, where you do not get what you want from life? Do you want to achieve a variety of goals, yet none have been realized? The reason for this could be that the will to achieve the objective or objectives is weaker than what restricts you. For example, if you want to be a successful entrepreneur, but get no closer to your goal, it may be that you have a variety of constraints which you let control your life. As long as the willingness to change is of secondary significance compared with the limitations, consciously or unconsciously, success will be absent.

The solution lies in having the intuition's help to set goals that you really want to achieve and to learn what limits you. Intuition is our inner, unlimited soul connection to God. We can use it to set goals and achieve them—by using your intuition, you can choose the life you want. Can we all use intuition? The answer is actually yes, but we have learned not to trust it and to instead rely on the environment. When we are born, we are intuitive and know exactly how to react and take action to get things to happen. But during our childhood, we are told to do so much that goes against our intuition that we finally turn it off. When we become adults, there is little or no intuition left, and we must rely on what others say and what our conditioned mind thinks is right. But if we all just trust in what others say, a better future is not created. The key to get back our intuition is to explore what we want deep down inside us and dare to focus on achieving it. With the help of your intuition, you can find out what your inner truth is so you can go from the point where you are now to where you want to be through changing your life. You can change your perception, your perception of yourself, by choosing not to see things relating to yourself in the way that others think you should see them, but seeing them as they are true for you.

But no intuition in the world will help you if you do not make an active change in your physical world. You must dare to affirm what you feel intuitively and actually write that book, start that company, or get rid of the phobia which you intuitively know how to solve, but the paradigm often is so strong that you are kept in old habit patterns so that no change occurs. Many are so stuck in conditioned thoughts and behavioral patterns that they do not trust their intuition. Often it is good if you come to a point where you no longer have any choice but to use your intuition, a point where there is no alternative but to really trust in this divine force within yourself. I myself had reached a point where I did not get anything out of life. There was no quality of life to mention, although I had lived for some years. My rational thinking, which was largely built on my mother's fears which had been conditioned inside of me, to a large degree unconsciously on her part, had created a life of resentment, self-loathing, and suicidal thoughts. My salvation was that I saw no alternative but to turn my life around. Admittedly, I could have committed suicide and become free that way, but for some reason I knew that this was no solution. Somehow I knew deep inside that I should hold on until I or someone else found the reason why I felt so bad. When

I finally realized that the answers would not come from someone else, I got access to my intuitive gift. All people have access to this intuitive gift. In most people it remains undetected, but everyone has the opportunity to bring it back to life. Either we continue using old, familiar, conditioned habit patterns, or we make a choice to really rely on and use our intuition. I sincerely hope that you do not have to experience the agonizing pain that I felt to do this choice, but for me and certainly for some others, it was the pain that was the beginning for a positive life. Now I am not saying that pain is necessary, but for me the inner pain is actually the reason why I write this book. The pain was the key to my intuition and to a life that I did not know existed, but I always wanted. The pain was the external symptom that I was heading the wrong way and had to change direction. Not that anyone forced me, but my inner truth wanted me to wake up from the torment in which I had allowed myself and others to violate me twenty-four hours a day. That was how it worked. Either my terrible conditioning made sure that I violated myself when I was by myself, or my self-image was mirrored by others, who then also violated me, directly, indirectly, consciously, and unconsciously.

This is how life is: we attract what we really believe about ourselves. It was certainly not my real truth, but my paradigm said it was my reality. Poor self-image and self-loathing always attract negative situations and people to you. It is not because God is evil, but that God wants to awaken our inner awareness and get us to dare to make a change. The external symptoms are only there because you should really wake up and take charge of your life and make a change so that you are starting to live your inner truth. The negative is actually positive. We have just decided that challenges and pain are something negative, while God wants us to use them for our development. Even those who do not have difficult challenges can obviously change their lives, but because they then do not have the same negative, external symptoms as rocket fuel, they must find another motivating factor to make the change. Pain can actually be the key to your true self. If you do not have so much pain in your life, it means you are closer to your inner truth and you do not need to make as much change to get where you want. The desire to change must always be stronger than the paradigm and the fear that keep you where you are; otherwise, no change is possible. Therefore, please make sure that what drives you to change is something you are passionate about. You need the inner will and strength to really do what you want. The force can not be created by someone else or bought for a price. You need to discover and create it within yourself. Remember that life is not a trial race. Decide right now to make the change you want to achieve. Change is really not at all dangerous, but the fear of being different and exposing ourselves to the risk of failure prevents many of us from doing what we want with our life. But you can only fail if you choose to see what happened as a failure. What others and you see as failures are perhaps just other steps towards your success. Instead see life as an opportunity to really challenge yourself so you can grow to the best you can be. These challenges, which others might see as failures along the way, are perhaps just what you need to succeed. Do not let yourself be broken by the taunts and harsh words of others, but make the best you can of life and free your self from their condescending views. For it's still up to you to live your life; no one will live it for you or through you.

Balance at all Levels

It is important to achieve balance on the physical, mental, emotional, soul, and spiritual levels in life. It is not enough to create external balance at the physical level with good finances, for example. Success is created from the inside out. This means that the more blocks you have deep inside, the less likely it is that you can achieve balance. You need to solve your challenges at each of the five levels. When you do this, you train your intuition all the time.

EXERCISE 5.1: *Become whole at all levels*

1. Write down the five levels. Here, I mean that you can draw an apartment building with five levels, where the top is the physical level, and under that you have the mental, the emotional, the soul, and finally the spiritual level, which is the foundation of your greatness.

2. Write down what percentage of your capacity you use at each level. I mean how much of your total ability to create balance you use on each level. Write down the answers that intuitively come to you.

3. If you had only 3 percent balance on the emotional level, you can, for example, ask yourself what is within you that lets you use only 3 percent of your capacity at this level. Write down the answers that come to you.

4. Trace the answers back to the underlying cause and find out where the block is locked in (time, event, feelings) with the Soulbalance method. Then you are free from the blockage and can change to achieve your inner truth.

5. Be patient—the process may take a while.

The best thing is obviously to have 100 percent capacity utilized at all five levels. But do not despair if it is not so right now. Heal what needs to be healed in order to obtain flow at each level. One might, for example, have full flow at the soul level, but have some challenges at the mental level. A belief that everything must be scientifically proven, for example, can be a block that you need to solve to get in touch with your intuition, which lies at the soul level.

Intuition versus Gut Feeling

There is a difference between intuition and gut feeling. The difference is that intuition is more of a sensation in both body and soul. The gut feeling reflects more how worried you are and how difficult everything is. It is based on your emotional conditioning and is linked to decisions confirming your conditioning. This means that when you follow your gut feeling, you make decisions which often are limited by fear and transferred from others to you. On the other hand, to make decisions based on the sensations you experience (that will come from your intuition) will help you act in direct contact with your inner truth. When the soul gives you advice in the form of sensations, you can create the life that your soul knows that you can create, no matter how scared your gut feeling says you are. The intuition is your link to your soul and the universal soul which makes it possible to re-create the balance you were born with. Only you yourself can make you happy. If you feel resentment and envy, let go of these destructive paradigms; they are not you, but something that you against your will inherited from someone else. Instead use your intuition to create things through your creativity. I myself carried bitterness and jealousy because I felt that my life was such hell. It was not until my intuition gave me the insight that my life is not a hell, although my inherited conditioning perceives it so, that everything fell into place. You are not your conditioning, although many others, and perhaps you yourself, choose to believe in it.

Why general Methods and answers do not work for everyone

Have you tried all methods and none of them helped? There is an explanation for this. We are individuals and therefore general advice does not work. Each individual is so unique that it would be an insult to everyone to be told there is one general method with its advice that would be the solution for everyone. With the Soulbalance method, there is admittedly a framework to get you started with your intuition, but to really succeed, you will adapt the method to your life and your circumstances. There is no general, intuitive response that fits us all. It's best to just get started and see where your intuition takes you. Dare to use it fully. You can even go beyond the framework and create your own solutions. Then it's just to congratulate you, as one purpose of the intuition is specifically to set you free from the collective thinking where others are talking about what is best for you. I was on a television program about coaching where I explained how I had healed myself with my intuitive method. One of the programs participants, a licensed psychologist (nothing wrong with the profession of psychology), believed it was not good that I had healed myself and helped others to heal themselves through my method. She thought that I should have sought additional help from traditional health care, where I admittedly had sought help for fifteen years without any results. Her attitude ridiculed each individual's own ability to make decisions about what is best for him or her. To assume that the method is correct and the individual is wrong is not what I stand for. With the intuition, the individual is right and the method is the tool for each individual's quest for his or her inner truth. We have come to a time when people have had enough of other people making decisions about their lives. The holistic approach, which looks to the whole individual, is coming, and science cannot stop this. People want to feel good and in control of their lives, whether it is scientific or not. Everything new is always a bit scary, as we unfortunately are conditioned with this attitude since childhood with a social inheritance ranging many generations back. But had no one dared to defy the standards, we would still believe that the earth is flat. Dare to trust your intuition no matter where it takes you, and do not let fear stop you. It is only the external symptom of your conditioning that will keep you in the old habit patterns where you feel comfortable and safe. But is it the real purpose of life that we should live in a comfort zone where we never challenge ourselves? Those who dare to live life fully are often the happiest people because they really have an outlet for their inner truth. An inner truth that is not manifested in physical form only creates frustrations and limitations. Time after time it has been shown that intuition is what determines our success in life. The greatest leaders are always using their intuition, because they generally do not have anyone to ask what is right or wrong. You can now also develop your intuition and create what you want in life.

EXERCISE 5.2: *Intuitive decisions in everyday life*

1. Imagine that you've decided to eat an apple, which you may do sometime.

2. Try now to put a bowl of fruit in front of yourself with, for example, apples, pears, oranges, bananas, and kiwis.

3. Instead of making a decision with the thought of which fruit you should eat, decide just what fruit you are drawn to, excluding your thoughts. The fruit you choose, you have then chosen with your intuition. Often we then choose a different fruit than the controlling habitual pattern says that we should choose.

In this case, I chose fruit, but you can use this exercise in all areas of life. You need "only" to build up and strengthen yourself so that you trust your intuition in all situations. You will receive both internal and external criticism for going your own way. But is not it better to go your own way, where you can achieve what you dream about, than to helplessly follow others to please them? This does not mean you cannot cooperate with others, but only that you put the focus on yourself to heal yourself. Then you can be in contact with other people and help them also.

Develop your intuition correctly

EXERCISE 5.3: *Intuitive timing determines everything*
Just as important as finding your intuition is developing it properly when you want to create change. This exercise will help you not only to make the right intuitive decisions but also to execute what you do with the right people and at the right time. If you intuitively chose the right thing to do, but have chosen the wrong partner or date, you will not have the success your intuitive decisions deserve.

1. *What should you do?* Feel intuitively and write down what you should do at work, in your leisure time, or in any other context you want to work with.

2. *When are you going do it?* Timing is everything. Feel intuitively and write down when it will happen. Do not let the limiting paradigm disturb you, but write down the true positive feelings that exist within you regarding this. Keep in mind that a correct intuitive decision can be understood as wrong when the timing is wrong.

3. *With whom should you do it?* Write down the names that come to you intuitively. Do not choose what your limited thought wants, but what you know deep inside is right for you. You can sometimes be surprised by the response you may get, but follow what has been given to you, as it is applicable. Do not hesitate, even though your limited paradigm will do everything possible to avoid a positive change for you.

I often get an intuitive response that does not seem reasonable rationally, but as long as I follow my intuition it will still always be right. I have chosen to always follow my intuition, no matter how strange the answers I get seem to be. My intuition has always taken me where I should be, while my conditioned thought has caused so many problems for me. Do you have a project that is right with the wrong person or persons? You know how wrong it will turn out.

4. *How will you implement the project?* Many projects will not succeed due to the lack of an action plan. Sit down and let the action plan flow to you intuitively, and write it down as it feels right for you. I always do this—for example, with this book project—and my intuition tells me how to go about it. If I were to trust the old familiar paradigms, including childhood traumas and memories, not much would be accomplished. I have, among other things, had a conditioning that says, "It makes no sense to try, because what if I do it wrong?" That paradigm, I definitely do not want as a part of my life. It sat so heavily rooted in me that it almost cost me my life, and it definitely ruined my joy of life. Using the Soulbalance method, I was able to liberate myself from the negative paradigms and start creating the life that I was destined, not conditioned, to live. To act using the intuition is of key importance.

You have probably, like me, made many decisions that you did not want to make or did not believe in, but for some reason you did not let your intuition be heard. Intuition is the soul's way to help you make contact with your inner truth. The soul knows what is right or wrong for you no matter what others say or what your paradigm says. How do you know if your intuition gives you the right answer? When you first start to train your intuition, most of us are still making decisions based on our conditioning. So in the beginning, many believe that their intuition gives them the wrong answer, but it is really their paradigm that still is making itself heard. The best and only way is to dare to trust your intuition. The more you trust it, the better it works. How do you know if it is right or wrong? It's simple: when it becomes what you want, it is right, but when it does not become what you want, it is based on your conditioning. I myself have been in doubt many times, but when I follow my intuition, it becomes right in the long term. At first it may look hopeless when the conditioning is doing everything to make itself heard and keep you in a mediocre state. But when you dare to let go of this short-term need for control, the intuition will bring you where you want. When things do not happen as you intended, do not see it as a failure, but as a step closer to your inner truth. Learn from your mistakes and reflect on when during the process you did not listen to your intuition. Realize that you must dare to try and dare to fail, otherwise you will never succeed. Too many people are overly afraid of not daring, for what if they might fail? If you are uncertain and insecure inside, you need to derive and resolve the cause of these feelings before you can create balance. Your internal and external self should be in balance with each other to make you feel good. Otherwise a conflict between the internal and external is created or maintained. The solution is to dare to fail while you solve your internal conflicts using your intuition. The more you dare, the stronger you become. Practice makes perfect. You will only end up where you want to be once you dare to face all your fears and paradigms. Sometimes it feels impossible to face oneself and one's conditioning. But once you have gone through the fear, your intuition strengthens further.

If you get Disconnected

If you have set a target and then get scared and start to think about what others will say and how it will work, you have probably set a goal that is in line with your inner truth. You are right on with your intuition, but your conditioning and others' opinions often want to say how wrong you are. We then often panic and rely on the advice from others and lose our greatest gift, our intuition. Also, a host of other restrictions may be in your way until you reach your goal, but by using your intuition according to the Soulbalance method, you can become aware of and handle them, thus creating the life you want. In some situations, you now have surely learned how to master your intuition, but for some reason you lose touch with it. This happens to most people sooner or later.

Finding your Way back to the Intuition

Understand that the intuition always has been there inside of you. You may have been unaware of it, but it is there, active or passive, in all people. You need to rediscover what you already have in you. If you do not feel that it has ever been inside you, then it is certainly your conditioning or other blockages that created this resistance. But be calm; all the clients I have worked with so far, and there are many who consider themselves intuitive hopeless, could find their intuition again regardless of what they thought about their intuitive abilities. If the desire to find it is there, you will find it. The points listed below can help you when your intuition falters. If you never have felt that you have intuition, you can use these points to create an initial contact and understanding of your intuitive ability.

• Have confidence that God is always there for you. God will not leave you just because your contact with your intuition temporarily disappears.

• Have confidence that intuition arises when you need it, neither sooner nor later. Intuition is a divine tool to help you get the development you need to grow to the best you can be. Do you have a need to control everything to the extreme? Your intuition will help you release these negative habit patterns. It is not always the most convenient for your conditioning, but it is the best for your soul that you create a sound approach, free from controlling needs, whatever your paradigm says.

• When it feels as if your intuition is gone, your soul often processes layers of old conditioning. When you "peel your onion" and start to unveil your inner truth, which is the center of the onion, you will have periods of processing when a lot of emotions need to be released from your paradigm. During these periods often all energy is spent on processing your emotions. Then there is neither the time nor space to search and especially not to check with your intuition. On the other hand, when you go through more peaceful and harmonious periods in your life, it is often the right time for new intuitive decisions and solutions.

• By this I mean that you will have periods when you feel that you can intuitively create what you want. You may feel as you are in some kind of flow where everything works out for you right now. But we are constantly in the flow, even when we feel that things do not go our way. With intuitive knowledge and with God's helping hand, miracles also happen when it feels the very hardest. When you work with the Soulbalance method, this can occur. You will switch between periods of total balance and freedom, and periods when your life feels heavy. Healing takes place in both of these situations, but it only feels positive when you fly through life. However, without the self-development you experience during the heavy part, you would not have access to the next, brighter part.

• So your journey will continue towards healing through layer after layer. Your divine contact and intuitive ability only intensify the more you peel away, but when you go through a blockage, it often does not feel this way. Do not worry. After rain comes sunshine, even if it many times may seem impossible and you just want to give up on everything. Sunshine in your life can come and will come whether you experienced it earlier or not. It is a fantastic feeling to help a client experience happiness for the first time with help of the Soulbalance method, and there have been a number of occasions when this happens in the collaboration between my clients and me. I am so happy and proud, but I actually know that it is God who is the power behind everything like this. That I may be part of this divine gift is reward enough.

• Do not forget that you will come out on the other side with more balance, more insights, and greater success. When you are in the middle of a period of processing, it may feel like you will die when you heal the current emotion, but hold out. Eventually you will be on the other side, and then you will let go of all thoughts of how difficult it just was.

• Remember that miracles take place every day, and that even you may be involved in this process.

Your conditioning will constantly challenge your intuitive decisions. The paradigm wants proof that everything you do is right and, in many cases, scientific evidence. The solution is to rely on your intuition even in situations when your paradigm denies what you do. To let go of the old familiar conditioning is perhaps the hardest thing you will ever do. Continue to be intuitive so that the paradigm eventually will give in and you can grow into the one you really want to be. The greater the divergence between the location that your paradigm says you are and where you really should be intuitively, the greater the resistance of this healing process. The resistance is just a sign that you are challenging your paradigms, solving them, and achieving your goals.

What happens when everything seems doomed and your intuition is just not there? When you are faced with hesitation, when doing an intuitive choice, you can do the following:

1. Your doubt means that you do not get the answers you should get. Decide, therefore, whatever your conditioning says, to fully rely on your

intuition. Confidence in your ability to trust your intuition allows you to grow as a person. Whatever happens with your answers, you will grow when you begin to rely on your intuition. Doubt arises as your rational thinking paradigm has a hard time believing that you can heal yourself with the help of God. Here it is of main importance to ride out the storm and trust that your intuition is with you. Going into doubt often destroys the unique divine contact that we have created. Do not let your conditioning or others' opinions ruin your intuitive ability. Keep in mind that your intuition will take you to a whole new positive level and give you a view of life that your rational conditioned thought never can give you.

2. Do not worry about what answers you get. Your worry is stopping you from creating the confidence you need. Trust the process and its answers.

3. Do you feel that the answer you get is right, but you are afraid? That means everything is completely in order. When you get intuitive answers, you often go against your conditioning that then faces it all with fear so that you will remain in the old habit patterns.

4. Make the next intuitive decision right now, and then the next and the next. Do not give up or quit just because your paradigm wants that. The paradigm can provide you with powerful symptoms when old negative blockages are cleared out, so be on your guard when they make themselves heard.

The soul is the intuition's search engine. Everything in your life is a reflection of your soul's image of yourself. Are you feeling bad? You need to consider how your soul is feeling. Do you have bad finances? You also need to examine how your soul feels. If you have it tough, it does not necessarily mean that there is something wrong with you. The soul wants to tell you something so that you can grow. If we get no symptoms in the form of, for example, poor finances, or depression, there is a risk that we do not create any change, but only let life roll on.

Divine flow

So the time has come when you really can use your intuition, 100 percent. You have learned the techniques to derive it according to the Soulbalance method and feel quite sure of yourself. Now it is time to really test your intuition fully. You stand at a crossroad where you can choose to follow the path outlined by your conditioning or choose the intuitive way. Now all belief in your intuition seems to have vanished and you feel doubt. What happens inside you is that old paradigms surface and try to determine how you should live your life. To really rely on your intuition, no matter how intense the condemning fear is, is an outward sign that you trust what God wants to communicate to you 100 percent. Do you dare to resist all external and internal criticism and do what is right for you and your soul? You will get so much back from God and the universe. It is not so much about the money and fame, but more about getting the opportunity to live a life that is completely free from the ego. You may on the surface be rich or poor, but inside you know you are acting free from the ego and in harmony with God. Do you make all decisions intuitively? Then the ego can have no power over you, for you live according to the divine flow.

Chapter 6

The importance of being Confirmed

There is hope for those who drink too much, for those who are fighting against obesity, those who cut themselves, and those who never experienced any serious external assault but still feel bad. Most people who feel unwell have not been through difficult experiences; they just have not gotten the love they need. But it is taboo to talk about this. Can you honestly say to yourself that you, from your childhood, have received so much love from your parents that you love yourself 100 percent? I cannot say it and have therefore had to give myself that love and self-affirmation. Children need to hear and feel that their parents love them—often. Otherwise it is not possible for a child to love himself or herself. True love is teaching the child that he or she can achieve anything in life. In order to give our children that, we need, as parents, to free ourselves from our own limitations. Love, however, should not be confused with overprotecting children or giving them a lot of things. The ability to give unconditional love should be a requirement for having children. To get unconditional love from our parents is such a gift that it frees us from the feeling of having to be good enough for others. Conditional love, which really is not love because it is based on requirements, can never give us or our children what we all need. Did you get unconditional love? Do you dare to invest in life regardless of external circumstances? If you have not received unconditional love, you can find it within yourself through the exercises in this book, which will help you get rid of your negative conditioning, layer after layer, until the soul is whole and your inner unconditional love for yourself surfaces. It has always been there; it has only been hidden deep below your conditioned desire to be good enough for others.

Unconditional love:

1. It means you have learned not to let yourself be influenced by others' opinions about what choices you make in life, but you have the courage to go your own way. If you do not have the courage to go your own way and are always looking for external confirmation from others, it may be the time to see how things are with your inner love for yourself. If you have not gotten the right encouragement during childhood, your life often will be just about living up to others' expectations.

2. The power of love is greater than all the fears that prevent you from becoming the best you can be. The more you work on your internal, unconditional love for yourself, the more power you create to go through the fears that limit you.

3. Love can be love for yourself, your children, your spouse, yes, everyone you want to share your vision and your life with. Once you have started to build your unconditional love for yourself through the Soulbalance method, you can even begin to spread it to others if you wish. It is nothing you must do, but you can give unconditional love to more than your children. But always start with yourself and your children. If you cannot give yourself that love, you have no ability to give it to others. I did not have it, because I felt that I had not received it

from my parents, which meant I did not understand what it was. I could not give it to my children seven to eight years ago. It was not until I began to heal myself with the Soulbalance method that my unconditional love for myself became true, and I had consequently developed my ability to give it to my children, whom I now love unconditionally.

As a coach I meet elite athletes, anorexics, alcoholics, IT millionaires, and other businesspeople that say that they do not feel that they are good enough. If you do not have the ability to love yourself and know that you are good enough, you need approval from the rest of the world. The most important quality to develop in ourselves and our children is self-esteem. With it you can move mountains. The soul is always on the lookout for situations in order to obtain approval if you have not received it in childhood. The problem is that the approval is inadequate if the soul does not get just the approval it needs to heal the wound. You can try to get approval from the rest of the world and maybe even get it, like a pop star, but if you have not been taught how to approve of yourself, you will in the depth of your soul never feel really loved. The basis for self-approval you need to get between birth and the age of seven. Until the age of seven or eight years old, the subconscious mind is fully open to external impressions. If your parents did not acknowledge you, if no one else affirmed you at all, damage to your soul occurred.
It is not just what your parents say, believe, feel, and think, but also what you know and feel about yourself that matters. At seven or eight years of age we begin to have a conscious self. If you have not been sufficiently affirmed by your parents and others around you, you will feel that you are not good enough. You then have both feelings and thoughts about

being unaffirmed. Children must be treated individually based on their soul balance, but of course parents must be as fair as possible towards the other siblings. One of your children may need more confirmation to know that he or she is good enough. Another needs more challenges to grow. If you treat your children the same, problems may arise. One of the kids grows up and thinks that life is fantastic, while the other feels really bad. It is important as parents to give children confidence in themselves to help them create the life they want. An imbalance between where we want to be and where we are creates anxiety. The basis for the imbalance is already created in childhood and therefore is it is important to treat the children individually.

The conditioning you get from your parents is strong, beginning at the *physical level.* If you never feel physical closeness with them, it becomes alien to have physical contact with others. I never got the physical touch and unconditional love I needed, and therefore fought with feelings of closeness to myself and others until I began to heal myself. On the *mental level* are the thoughts that tell you that you are not good enough, and these thoughts leave an imprint on your *feelings.* The paradigm in the soul then says that you are not worthy to exist, that you live very far from your inner truth, and that problems occur at the *soul level.* This in its turn means that the *spiritual* contact begins to shut down.

The law of Attraction

If you do not deep down love yourself, you will attract situations where you do not feel loved and satisfied, all according to the law of attraction. A child who has not been sufficiently acknowledged sends out vibrations that make him or her fail often, and because of that he or she will be even more criticized and feel more unconfirmed. Some become perfectionists; many feel very bad. But it is possible to become whole again. Traditional thinking according to the law of attraction says that you will attract what you think. So if you think success and balance, you will get this. I believe that the law of attraction attracts what your conditioning thinks of you, which then becomes something entirely different. I never received what I thought until I had become free of my negative paradigms using the Soulbalance method. Until then, I just attracted everything my conditioning believed to be true. There was self-loathing, anger, grief, poverty, and so much more. These paradigms created no balance or success no matter how successful I tried to think. Once I had solved my soul blockages, I attracted the new true soul image of myself, free from negative paradigms.

If you never get confirmation that what you are doing is good enough, you must constantly achieve more to have the chance to hear that you are loved. This can lead to perfectionism and controlling disorders. If you do not feel love inside, you try to create the recognition from the outside by performing perfectly, dressing perfectly, and so on. It can create a temporary satisfaction, but the feeling of not being loved will always come back. People who love themselves never will violate themselves and thereby will not harm themselves. For example, all types of abuse are self-abusive. The basic reason for the abuse needs to be derived and solved and the external behavior adapted to the new situation. To merely change the behavior is not enough, because the inner unresolved cause only manifests itself in a different external

symptom. This you often see when, for example, a sober alcoholic creates other obsessive behaviors to numb his or her anxiety, and the other behaviors have the same basic cause as the alcohol abuse.
When you set up goals in life, your subconscious mind, which consists of both the emotional and soul levels, looks for recognition. When you are used to feeling unaffirmed, it will manifest in your results. When you have got this feeling of being unaffirmed into your subconscious, it will be perceived as the truth. Then you can try anything, such as yoga, meditation, or reading books about self-help, but it is not until the soul cause is derived and solved that the healing can occur. There are usually seven to eight basic situations that damage our sense of self during childhood. These can then take the form of thousands of negative expressions in our life. One can call them symptoms due to a lack of affirmation. Just as you have symptoms on the physical plane, in the body, or in the form of poor finances, you can also have them on the mental and emotional levels. The feeling of not being affirmed in childhood is not about what your parents say they did or said. It is all about the child's experience. Every child is unique in his or her soul constitution and has unique needs. We come to earth as soul beings. This means that two children in one family can have two completely different needs of approval and very different challenges facing them in life. My parents never told me that they loved me. My mother gave me tea in bed, but never said she loved me. The lack of affirmation meant I had low self-esteem and developed severe anxiety.

I tried mental training for fourteen to fifteen years, I tried to be good in sports, tried to exercise control by being the best in school, suppressing the emotions, but nothing helped. What I discovered was that no type of therapy where someone else takes responsibility for my life would help me.

My soul is here to enrich people, to help them become the best they can be and achieve their dreams. But I was born into a family where the signals sent out were about "you cannot, be cautious, others are better, they succeed, what if you fail, you are not good enough." This was not just what my parents said, but also how they perceived life. Everything I loved to do—the creativity with the theatre, drawing, working as a model, being good in sports—there was no approval. My soul wanted to create its own inner truth. But in the end I was living life as a copy of my parents. Living under these conditions was so far from my inner truth that I developed a severe anxiety condition that lasted many years. The solution is to release this pain, replacing it with a huge self-assurance about oneself. For some people, the lack of love from their parents remains hidden for quite some time. But sooner or later it will surface, because the soul strives for you to live according to your internal truth, and you cannot do that as long as you do not love yourself.

Affirm Yourself

There are four types of affirmation. The first is to be affirmed by one's parents, to feel and know that you are good enough no matter what you do with your life. You are good enough just being here on earth. This affirmation most parents cannot provide—not that they do not want to, but because they have not been affirmed themselves. You cannot give something you never had. The second type of affirmation is the affirmation you give to yourself. The third kind of affirmation comes from others, and the fourth is the affirmation that comes from God. The ideal is to get affirmation on all four levels. But if you do not have that, you can heal yourself by affirming yourself and being affirmed by God.

If you have not received affirmation from your parents, you do not know how to affirm yourself. Work with yourself using the Soulbalance method until you feel total internal affirmation. Then it can replace the feeling that you have not received affirmation from your parents. Once you experience affirmation from yourself and begin to set goals, you will also want to get outside affirmation. Your internal affirmation is seeking external expression according to the law of attraction. This means that when you acknowledge and love yourself, you will be drawn to situations where you get external affirmation and vice versa. One example is a person who is beaten up in her or his relationship and leaves that partner, but then gets into another destructive relationship. If the person is able to change her or his self-image and be self-affirming, she or he will next time get a partner who shows respect. If you actually have affirmed yourself but have not invested in the external manifestation of the affirmation, you will not experience total balance in life. It is not that you must be good enough for other people. External affirmation is confirmation that you have created the internal balance. They do not come together, but they go hand in hand.

EXERCISE 6.1: *Heal yourself from feeling unaffirmed*

1. Look at what wounds or symptoms of damage you have. An external symptom may be that you do not feel affirmed by other people at a

party. Use the Soulbalance method and look at where the symptom comes from as mentioned below.

2. Trace back by examining when the damage occurred. Is it in this life, past lives, or in the creation energy? Write your thoughts down and circle what feels intuitively right for you.

3. If the blockage is derived from this life, write down the age when you intuitively feel that the damage occurred. If the blockage is traced back to past lives or the creation energy, you do not need to find any dates. Dates are not important to solve the challenge there, but if you discover a connection to a particular year, it can of course not cause any harm.

4. Derive what happened.

5. Are any people involved? Who are they and what is their part in the whole thing? (This paragraph does not apply to the creation energy.)

6. Then, it is important to find the restrictive, negative feelings that are there. The blockages which remained hidden in the soul will be released. God helps you in this healing process.

7. Once you have done this, you have solved the soul cause. Then you just need to create situations where you are not affirmed, but where you give yourself the affirmation. The reason for this is because we have already solved the blockage on a deeper level, but unless you change the behavior the healing will not be complete. When you also are

manifesting your release of your internal blockage with an external action confirming your new inner free image, you can create new, positive external behavior patterns.

Say you have always been afraid that you are not good enough. You resolve this conditioning and now know deep down that you are good enough, but you still have negative thoughts, feelings, and behavior patterns. Manifest this new internal security with actions that you deserve, in this case, for example, by treating yourself to sleep late Saturdays no matter what your mother-in-law thinks about this. She is in this case conditioned to find that you are lazy if you sleep late on the weekend. You are now in balance and can do what is right for you and not what someone else's conditioning wants you to do. It is not enough merely to make the internal change, just as it is not enough to simply make an external change. The solution is to make both an internal and an external change to get positive, lasting results. Your internal and external changes account for the same thing, and success is a fact. After a while, you are so secure in yourself that you will be automatically affirmed.

Free yourself from the need for affirmation from others

A major problem in our society is that everyone is seeking affirmation from others to feel good enough. This means that no one does what is right for them, but everyone is trying to be good enough in the eyes of other people. During my childhood my need for approval was so great that I would stay home the whole weekend if I had a pimple on my nose or if I had been turned down by a girl. This may seem trivial, but such was my reality. I had no self-worth at all, so the days were passed chasing affirmation from others. When you start solving your soul blockages, you will sooner or later come to the realization that you are good enough no matter what others think about you. Now you can live the life you want, rather than simply being good enough for someone else. We cannot and need not be loved by everyone. If you love yourself and know that you are good enough for the whole, God, that is enough. You do not need to be forgiven by God to be good enough, for you are always good enough in God's eyes. If you are struggling with that or you feel you have done wrong against someone else in any respect, you are still good enough in God's eyes. What we need to do is to forgive ourselves for the acts that are not ethically correct, not according to the rules others have, but in relation to our own internal code of ethics. If violations occur, and the internal ethics do not stop them, then surely the individuals who violate their own ethics have developed a protection mechanism to guard against the negative feelings that are threatening them in the subconscious mind. Often such people have psychopathic behavior, which includes a lack of empathy and inability to show emotions. Even these people can heal themselves—but only if they really want to. Have you thought about how much we are doing to make others happy, happy with us, or anything else that will help them, but puts us off track? Then you are not alone. In today's society, it is so foul to think about oneself first that almost everyone is walking around with a bad conscience from feeling that they are not good enough for others. Would it not be better to first take care of oneself to enjoy life and be happy with what one does and who one is, instead of running around the whole world trying to be good enough for others? In these destructive habit patterns many problems stem, including anorexia, poor self-image, and self-destructive thoughts and behavior. It is also why so many models, actors, and celebrities feel so bad. They want to be good enough for others instead of feeling good enough regardless of what others think of them. To build yourself up and be proud of who you are, regardless of what others think, is the foundation for feeling good. Then you do not have to ask yourself if you are good enough all the time, or wonder if you are nice enough or something else someone might think about you. The motto is: Live life so that you are impressed with yourself, instead of living a life where you need affirmation from the outside world's view that you are good enough. It is of course wonderful that others appreciate you, but you should not really be dependent on other people's opinions. When you feel affirmed in yourself and in your relationship with God, you have opened up the possibility to realize your dreams and to create balance in life.

To be affirmed by God

When you feel uncomfortable and feel that you have not gotten and do not get affirmation from your parents and your environment, you can always go back to the belief in the wholeness, in God, and then even in yourself. God will always support you and you can withstand a lot, although others say that you are not good enough. Just relax in the certainty that there is something greater than yourself that supports you when you need help.

To be affirmed by God can be summarized in five points:

1. Everyone is good enough for God regardless of what others think.

2. Everyone is good enough for God regardless of what you think.

3. Everyone is good enough for God regardless of what any religion says.

4. No one has sinned too much to be not good enough for God.

5. We all have the opportunity to take advantage of the intuitive and healing power with which God has endowed us.

I have coached individuals who have had challenges in one or more of the above areas, and no one has been denied the help of God, regardless of circumstances. However, what is needed for affirmation and healing is that the individual has:

1. a desire for positive change;

2. an openness to receive God's healing power.

Chapter 7

How to make your Paradigm shift

I heard it extensively as a child: "Hans, it is not possible to make money as a model. Hans, it is only possible for others. Hans, it is not possible. Hans, stop dreaming." Many in my class became successful. Why did they grow into success, but not me? If you have been conditioned since childhood that everything is impossible, it will be tough to live. When I grew up, I had only one thing in my head, and that was to be good enough. I felt like the least valuable person on earth. To feel that way creates serious problems. This means that we repeatedly fail, as our whole energy system is set so that we cannot succeed. What our parents think and feel is passed on to us. What they think and feel about themselves and show with their body language is important. These things condition us more socially than what they say. We carry these paradigms with us through life and, in our turn, transfer them to our own children. Paradigms can proceed through generations. They can take the form of being conditioned that wealth is something natural and something you can achieve, or it can be a constant feeling that everyone can achieve wealth, but not me. To be conditioned that wealth is something you can achieve does not mean that you are in balance as a whole and feel confirmed as a human. I have been able to help many individuals who have had allergies, depression, poor finances, poor health, and low self-esteem, which is inherited. One can look for genetic defects, but the social conditioning is so strong and goes from generation to generation so that it almost seems to become genetic. Often, the feelings of inferiority and despair cause all sorts of symptoms which are carried generation to generation through conditioning and automatically transferred to the child whether he or she wants them or not. Children have a wide open subconscious mind that takes up all the things that the parents stand for without being able to critically examine whether they want the information or not.

One way to get rid of one's negative conditioning and understand it yet better is to distance oneself from it—to take a step outside oneself and actually see the conditioned person one has become. Many of us are running around with a smile on our face even though we are full of self-loathing. But finally reality catches up with us and our inner self-loathing makes itself heard twenty-four hours a day. No matter what facade you put up, you feel worthless deep inside. I had through the years idealized my parents. Although I was feeling very bad, I could never believe that it was due to my conditioning. When I started to work intuitively, I got the advice from God to truly examine my life in a completely objective manner, which can only be done through pure intuition when one frees oneself from the ego's intentions and blockages. What I to my great horror discovered was how much negativity I had gotten from my parents. My mother is a person who makes sure that everything looks good on the surface, but underneath the polished surface she is very frustrated. It is always too hot, too cold, too windy, or something else that she sees as negative and she lives out her conditioning as a victim. She unfortunately brought her heavy burdens and fears over to me. Usually it is the most sensitive child who becomes an emotional wastebasket for the feelings that the other family members carry on. My mother really did not mean to be mean, but because of her conditioning she did not know better. I later noticed that my negative conditioning also affected my children very negatively. It was not until I began to heal myself and my negative conditioning with the Soulbalance method that they also began to feel better. As a parent, this awareness is crucial for your and your children's future balance and happiness. If the soul and its inner truth become very offended during childhood, often by people who are close to you, you begin to perceive this as the truth. The solution as an adult is to begin to sort out what is really true for you and what is learned by conditioning. This is a process that can take a while, but eventually you will live your internal truth.

At the same time that you begin to find your paradigms and derive them to their origin and solve them, a growth process starts that is of major importance. The development you go through is often equally as important as getting rid of the original block, and in this process a major part of the self-healing occurs. Health depends on *how* you process information, not only *what kind of* information you are processing. This means that two individuals can get exactly the same information but process it completely different, depending, among other things, on their various paradigms. With the right attitude and trust in your intuition, you can solve everything regardless of what your conditioning and external circumstances say. It is not what happens in your life that determines your situation, but how you perceive what is happening. This means that a child may have perceived his or her childhood as very negative but the parents think they did everything right. If the child perceives it as negative, that is the conditioning that the child will get regardless of what the parents think. In my case, my parents were convinced that they did everything right, instead of being aware of how I reacted to my environment. I was, for example, forced to start attending a school that I refused to go in, and I was thrown in a swimming pool by the swimming teacher to teach me how to swim at the age of five. But I sank like a stone, which traumatized me. My parents defended themselves afterwards by saying to me, when I was an adult, that they just did what the authorities and the school said. But they did so regardless of the consequences it had for me. I believe that their primary responsibility should be to ensure that I was not violated, while they felt that their responsibility was primarily to follow others' instructions. They did so without knowing better; they had no awareness of how damaging this was for me. But I got hurt for what I thought was life until I found the Soulbalance method, which can even heal these traumas' negative impact.

Live your life as you want

The realization that what we have experienced in life is optimal to give us the growth opportunities we need is relieving. It allows us to go from being a victim to having a more understanding way, where we realize that what we have experienced was necessary for us to reach the point where we are today. That does not mean that it is fantastic to have setbacks, but they can be of great value. This is difficult to recognize when you are in the midst of a crisis. But the healing insight that often comes after the crisis offsets the pain by a wide margin. I have a child with Down syndrome. The news put me in a crisis; the pain and sense of failure were devastating. Now I can look in the rearview mirror and see that without my daughter's disability, I would never have dared to let go of the feeling of trying to be good enough for others. With such a visible disability, one always stands out from the crowd and people often keep their distance. After a few years it gave me the motivation to venture and improve my life where I had no need to try to be good enough for others. I was now somehow free to do what I really wanted. Others' expectations no longer influenced me. Live your life as you want, free from your paradigm. Do not wait on a catastrophe but make the change now. The longer your conditioned life is spent away from your inner truth, the more powerful external signals you get, so you realize that change must happen. And the longer you wait, the stronger the external, negative symptoms will be. If and when a crisis arises, it is often just the tip of an iceberg consisting of years of internal humiliation in which we directly and indirectly allowed ourselves to be violated by ourself and others. Often, negative paradigms are a pattern of endless violations which are not always visible to us or others. But they are there. Society has, at best, crisis hotlines for victims of violence and rape. But no help has been there for the huge group of people who daily are violated by words and actions. The violations prevent us from being the best we can be in unity with God. That we have not been affirmed as children is often ignored by us and by our environment. But if we are sensitive enough, the violations can damage more than what our minds can understand. These symptoms can appear as anything from poor finances to poor health and relationships. This is the main reason for poor health in the developed countries. When so much of the population is not living their own life, but a life that is adapted to be good enough for others, then the history of negative paradigms has gone too far. Remember if you do things that go against your inner truth, it is in fact a violation, regardless of whether you and others perceive it to be or not. If you start an education to make your parents happy, it is an inner violation, if you really want to do otherwise.

But this can be solved. The solution is both simple and complex. Begin simply to derive and solve the basic causes of your negative conditioning with the Soulbalance method. Anyone can do it, but if you are conditioned in an extremely negative way, it can feel like looking for a needle in a haystack. But the improvement and healing will come, and the process is completely individual. The more you trust your faith in God, the easier it will go. Some may get total relief after a few sessions deriving and healing problems, while for others it may take considerably longer before results are visible. Do not be concerned about how it goes for others. Your development applies to you. Note the visible results, for the soul healing takes place immediately now that you are using the Soulbalance method. Sometimes we need more time to manifest what we have solved, and sometimes we need less time, depending on what lessons we need to get us on the way to the external balance and success. Do you have a paradigm of negativity from your childhood? You will easily get negative results when you are an adult. Maybe you have not been a victim of something negative in childhood, but still have negative results, or, on the other hand, maybe you have been surrounded by negativity, yet you may get positive results. Then the soul's conditioning that you carry from past lives, and in some cases from the creation energy, is much stronger than the conditioning you grew up with.

Therefore, there are people who can cope with difficult things, even if it looks bad on the surface, and others will be broken down even if things look good on the surface.

EXERCISE 7.1: *Replace the negative with the positive*

1. Ask yourself if you love yourself 100 percent. If you love yourself you do not care about what people think. If you answer no, find out what it is on the outer plane in your life that is making you not feel well. Write a list of things that are related to why you do not love yourself; for example, "afraid to make a speech." It may be a short list or a list of as many as twenty to forty points.

2. The feeling of not loving yourself goes back to the feeling that you are not good enough deep inside, that you do not love yourself in the soul. Explore it through the Soulbalance method: At what age did the feeling occur? What happened? When you find the underlying situation or cause, you will directly know intuitively that it is right and God will help you to heal.

3. Replace the negative feeling with the affirmation "I love myself all the time." An affirmation is a positive sentence written in the present tense which you read for yourself between five and ten times a day during about three weeks' time, for that is how long it often takes to change the conditioned negative feeling into a positive, even if the soul cause is resolved on the soul level through the Soulbalance method. If you do not love yourself as a child and during your adolescence, it is easy to perceive your conditioning as your inner truth. The paradigm then

controls your life as if it was you, when it really only suppresses and destroys your inner truth.

Look at your childhood. Did your parents love themselves? If they did not love themselves, they could not love you fully. Therefore, it is our obligation as parents to teach ourselves to love ourselves, so we can teach our children to love themselves. It is not what you say to your child about yourself but what you feel and radiate around yourself that determines how your child feels. The universe is great, the earth is great, we all have possibilities. If we could learn to love ourselves and teach our children to love themselves, there would be no war and no murders. Many children who are diagnosed with Attention Deficit Hyperactivity Disorder (ADHD) would feel good if they only had the opportunity to love themselves, and the prisons would not be so full. The problems are external symptoms of internal imbalances.

Self-esteem versus Self-confidence

Have you wondered why some people seem to be so secure in themselves while others are in such an imbalance? Why is this so? Often it has to do with our self-confidence and our self-esteem. The difference between self-esteem and self-confidence is that when you have good self-esteem, you love yourself no matter what happens. Self-confidence is based on what you create, for example, good finances or a good performance. Self-confidence can come and go, but self-esteem should be consistent. No money in the world can buy self-esteem; money only reinforces what you believe about yourself. Are you rich but you hate yourself? Money just makes you hate yourself even more. Many stars show this, having lots of money but also all too often a self-destructive lifestyle. One can live with the shortcomings of low self-esteem for a long time without showing any external symptoms. But sooner or later the illusion will burst, in the same way as a water pipe is damaged by rust. Your inner rust, poor self-esteem, then shows itself in external symptoms that you need to derive, process, and resolve in order to regain balance. If the conditioning associated with lack of love does not appear when we are children, it will, guaranteed, make itself heard when we come into adolescence. Then, many of us have a strong sense of not fitting in, not being good enough. If you have taught your child to love himself or herself, the child needs not drink too much alcohol, take drugs, and follow other destructive group behavior to feel good enough. The child *knows* that he or she is good enough.

Throughout school, many children feel that they must perform to be good enough for their parents, that they must live up to their parents' expectations and follow their conditioned path. But if children know they are loved, they can dare to choose another education than the parents had planned, because the children know that their parents love them no matter what course in life they chose. Give your children unconditional love; love them the most when you think they deserve it the least. Do not put conditions on your love, and do not let it flow just in good times when the child looks and performs in a way that makes you happy. Give the teenage girl love when she comes home with bad grades or looks like hell, and not just when she is perfectly dressed and has received passing grades. Praise and love her even when she passed the ball wrong lots of times during the game or when your son forgot to wipe the dinner table. Let love always be present, like a warm, comfortable undercurrent in touch with your children, and others' children as well. See them for who they are, not the people you want them to be. The feeling of always wanting to be good enough but never feeling that you are will haunt you if you do not do anything about it. Problems will come, first at school, then at work, and of course when you are going to be in a relationship. If you do not love yourself, you will probably find a partner who does not love himself or herself. It often leads to a destructive relationship, in one way or another, perhaps through jealousy, feeling less worthy, or being dominated. People who love themselves never let a partner treat them poorly but would rather break up. The negative love image you carry on attracts just a bunch of garbage: bad jobs, bad relationships. Then maybe you have children, and they are not given a chance to love themselves. You may succeed in getting out the "love" word, but the feeling behind it is missing. In this way the problems may continue from generation to generation, and this creates a lot of human suffering.

Get out of your Comfort Zone

To begin the journey towards loving yourself, you need to get out of your comfort zone, a state of "feeling sorry for yourself." You may have become conditioned to feel that you are not good enough. In the end, this conditioning will be seen as your normal self and will be included in your comfort zone without it necessarily being right for you. It is the comfort zone that accounts for the often misleading gut feeling, for it says "stay here to be sure" when you really should take yourself away from your negative security. You can do this if you trust your intuitive ability. If you have been stuck long in a negative comfort zone, it is also easy to feel sorry for yourself. You or I do not want to feel sorry for ourselves just for the sake of it, but we feel sorry for ourselves because of the crippling negative paradigm which keeps us in this particular zone. Do you not want to take yourself out of this? To reprogram yourself, you need to find out where you are now and where you really want to be.

EXERCISE 7.2: *To transform the negative into the positive*

1. Write down on a piece of paper how you have it now, both the positive and negative. Circle what is negative. Now you know what you have to change. Now take another piece of paper and write down where you want to find yourself in a year. Write down an exact date when you will have achieved your goal. Write in the present tense and with positive sentences free of negativity, so that your internal self perceives this as a positive truth already.

2. Transform the circled, negative things into something positive. Write next to each item you want to change an affirmation, for example: "I am successful at work," "I am happy in my relationship," "I weigh x pounds." Make sure you focus on finances, health, and relationships.

3. Now summarize the goals from the paper onto a goal card which you can always carry with you. The goal card makes you start to associate yourself with the card's contents at all times. The card must be written in present tense and free from any negatives. It should contain at least one measurable financial goal, a health goal, and a relationship goal (yours and others, if you wish). It may look like this: "By _________ (date), I am

so grateful that I have a company that grosses x number of dollars. I train at least twice a week and have at least x number of hours of quality time with my family/partner/friends (depending on how you live) a week." I have chosen to write the word "grateful" on all my goal cards to really manifest my gratitude to God when I create what I want and have the ability to achieve. It is absolutely not necessary to have any rituals, but a word of gratitude reinforces everything you write on the card. Create success without taking God's helping hand for granted. A certain amount of internal and external humility gives you the best results.

4. Read the card at least ten times morning and evening. The very best way is to do this in front of a mirror so you really are confronted with what you say on many levels. What you read that is not perceived as true for you will be bombarded with criticism from your paradigm. By reading the card over and over again, you will break down the negative conditioning that prevents you from reaching your goals. Finally your system realizes at four levels (mental, emotional, soul, and spiritual) that your goal is true for you, and achievable. Once that happens, it is only a matter of time before it is manifested on the physical level.

5. Also make an action plan, from the big things you need to do each year to the actions you have to do each month and week. Then make a list of what you need to do the next day to get closer to your goals. This list should contain at least six points. The list may, for example, look like this:

- Make two telephone calls.
- Sign a contract.
- Run x number of miles.
- Work one hour on my self-esteem.
- Help the children with homework.
- Treat the family to a restaurant visit.

6. Plan the actions at a level that suits you. We are all different and need various challenges. Do what feels intuitively right for you.

7. We are often so negatively conditioned by feeling that we are not good enough that we do not do what we should or what we need to do to achieve our goals. With this six-point list you challenge yourself to really make the external changes that are necessary for you to achieve what you want.

8. When you encounter resistance—maybe you are afraid to make a crucial telephone call—you can reflect on why. Perhaps you fear that the one you are calling is going to say no to what you want to ask for? What feeling does that raise in you? That you are not good enough? Trace the feeling to the soul level and you will probably find that you do not love yourself. Derive when that feeling came (intuitively find the right age) and the situation that caused it. Replace the negative feeling with the affirmation that you love yourself, and start to heal yourself.

You will experience a large amount of resistance because we are habitual creatures. Now you must leave your comfort zone and do things you are not are used to. The change will be gradual, and it comes through when you start to act towards the goals you have set. Dare to leave your passivity and create the life you want. Are you are experiencing burnout or uncertainty? Change direction and seek the solution. So many try to reduce stress, often as medical advice, but as long as you do not create the life you want, the symptoms will come back as soon as you start to work again. It is so obvious and so simple, yet so many of us go in the trap over and over again. You know the answer; act in the direction that your intuition tells you no matter what others think about it. Accept advice from others, but make decisions with your intuition, for it is you who have the responsibility for your life.

Violations

A huge group of individuals show physical symptoms of anxiety, self-contempt, and more without traditional health care being able to find any reason for their problems. If we do not get the attention that our soul needs when we are growing up, we can develop physical symptoms as strong as if they were caused by a much more serious problem. The problem is that if the soul feels offended, then severe symptoms develop, even if everything looks good on the surface. It explains why many feel bad even though no injury or other trauma can be detected. The soul only says that this is an unfair treatment that it is not willing and able to endure. One can be violated in so many different ways, such as assault, threats, or anything else around you that can be seen and that can be addressed when detected. It is not only these violations we are talking about, but the quiet, almost unnoticed violations that may continue for several years, even for decades. Such internal violations are probably among the worst things you can encounter. They paralyze the entire soul so that we cannot resolve anything that keeps us from our inner truth. If you were injured in this way as a child, when nothing or very little of what you did was good enough in your parents' eyes, then it is no wonder that you feel uncomfortable as an adult. It is a direct result of this. The astonishing thing is that it does not always affect all children in a family, so it does not only have to do with what the child is exposed to, but perhaps especially how the child perceived his or her upbringing. If you have had a childhood in which your soul feels offended and has not experienced what it needs, the external symptoms will eventually show so that you should be able to change direction and the soul get what it needs. For a child it is hard to see this, so to increase one's awareness of what the children in one's environment need to feel good is of highest priority. Are you a parent? Make sure that you give your children the love they need so that they can develop into the people they are intended to be, and not what you want them to be.

Are you a love-damaged adult who does not like yourself? Healing can never come from a parent's words and actions; you must learn to heal yourself in your relationship with God.

• A violation is when something is perceived as an infringement on your soul.

• Make sure no one violates you.

• If someone violates you, act so that the violation cannot continue.

• Take a look at your life and see what activities you do that violate you. It can be anything from going to a party you do not want to go to, to following a diet that you do not want to follow.

• Remember that you, as an adult, always choose how you act in your life. Let no one else decide how you should live your life.

Reconciliation

When you start to love yourself, you can feel contempt for your parents not having given you the love you needed. A variety of feelings which lay hidden can come up. But with the love for yourself, the understanding will also come. Parents have not, in most cases, acted intentionally. They have simply not been able to do more, as they have not learned to love themselves. Eventually the contempt disappears. Perhaps it is that you should not socialize with them, if it makes you feel bad. But the contempt is going to be released. Always forgive yourself because you have carried on these negative feelings. Often, we try to forgive others, but a great anger is directed towards ourselves for what has happened, whether it is our fault or not. You are never dependent on others in a forgiveness process, so you need to just forgive yourself because you carry anger and hatred. Forgiving oneself for what happened is crucial in many healing processes. With abuse, for example, the rape victim often feels guilty and dirty. Many therapies deal with how to forgive the person who made the assault. But it rarely works fully. When I started working with the process of reconciliation with the aggrieved, which included everyone from rape victims to individuals who never felt loved, I noticed that those who forgave themselves for carrying the negative feelings got a very strong healing process independent of others. When you forgive yourself for everything negative you carry around, the spiritual level goes in and helps you. Suddenly, you have gained access to God's healing power that supports you in all situations. When you forgive yourself for all the pain you carry, you realize that you are good enough, whatever your paradigm says. For your inner truth to be able to show—it has been embedded in thoughts, behavior patterns, and emotions—a lot of emotions must be allowed to surface. It may involve much physical, emotional, and mental pain, but it is a part of the self-healing process. Simply suppressing your true self is not working. It can lead to disease and depression. I have seen people heal from serious illnesses and poor finances by applying this method. I have seen everything. What you suppress, you will attract anyway. So have you suppressed a feeling of being worthless? You attract people and situations that reinforce the feeling, according to the law of attraction. In the end the feeling is so reinforced that you are still forced to change to reach your internal truth. You feel that you have no choice to get the results you want. Then you release your need for control that locks the negative image of you and your life. In my life, it is a striking example that I hated myself, and then got my handicapped child. Not that a disability is wrong, but because I needed a handicapped child to know that I never will be seen as good enough in others' eyes with all the prejudices that exist. I decided then that we as a family are good enough, whatever I myself and others think, which was a tremendous tool for self-healing. Now I have taught myself to love myself and to attract success, which also includes my daughter.

Flow between the Five levels

In order to get flow in life, you need to have the flow between the five levels. Just doing some occasional work on the five levels, each one individually, does not produce a whole. For some reason, we believe that we can have balance in our life without having it on all levels. All levels are interdependent, and the smallest imbalance or ignorance at any level will eventually show at every level. If a single response works, it is often that it is the last link in your puzzle, or the positive result is just temporary until all levels get the time and understanding they need. I show how with two examples: Ann has long struggled with being overweight. She goes to a gym to get help at the physical level, and to a coach to learn how to think right about food. But she still does not succeed in losing any weight on a long-term basis. If she loses weight, she sooner or later will regain her weight again. But if she goes in through the five levels and finds the reasons why she fails, she will succeed. She needs learn to love herself by affirmations. When she loves herself, she does not want to treat herself badly by eating in a way that is not good for her. By deriving the soul cause, all healing can take place in combination with an affirmation that confirms where she wants to be: "I love myself and am in balance with my weight."

Peter is a successful CEO, with a family he loves. But he does not feel really good, even though he on the surface has everything he could wish for. The problem is that he does not love himself. If he intuitively explores what level his injury is at and when it emerged, he can do affirmations and self-heal to find the true joy in life. Some need to reach rock bottom before they take hold of their life and find love for themselves. So it was for me. I was really in trouble before I seriously began to tackle the cause of my problems. But even if you have an okay life and are semisatisfied with living, you have everything to gain by learning to love yourself, so you will not look back on your life when you are eighty years old and regret that you have not lived fully. And if you have children, you can, when you love yourself, teach them to love themselves, and then chances are they will follow their inner truth. The farther down you have been, the more power you can create to actually self-heal. If you have not had so many challenges, you need less power to heal. The closer you are to your inner truth and the more your parents have supported you so that you can live closer to your inner truth, the fewer challenges you will have.

Stop being a Victim

What is certain for those of us who have been taught that everything is impossible is that we have a huge incentive to take ourselves from the situation where we are a victim to a position where we begin to heal. The worse it has been, the more power you most likely have, but you must stop seeing yourself as a victim. I had to take myself from being a victim to being an intuitive decision-maker to be free. With my victim mentality, I saw myself as unworthy and useless, and I was ready to get rid of these feelings. Using the Soulbalance method, I was able to gradually release the negative victim mentality and create the life I wanted. Do you not recognize yourself as a victim? All of us have to some degree the victim mentality in us when we feel sorry for ourselves. It may be because we did not get that job, because we did not lose weight, because we were not invited to the party. So what should we do not to be a victim? Nobody really wants to be a victim though the conditioning often keeps us there with all the benefits it can give us, or if you are a victim, you need not to take responsibility. If you are a victim, everything is someone else's fault. But only you can live your life, and it is only you who can give up your victim mentality and take responsibility for your life. Write down what you need to develop to take you from where you are to where you want to be, to go from a victim to actually be true to yourself and take responsibility for your life. I have myself been a victim, and I know how difficult it is to break this paradigm. I tried for almost forty years before the Soulbalance method gave me the tools I needed to get rid of the victim conditioning and all the damage my parents' victim mentality had caused me. You can get ride of the damage, too. You are good enough. Actually, you are no victim.

EXERCISE 7.3: *To go from victim to decision maker*

1. What are the qualities you need to develop to become free from being a victim? Write down four things that intuitively come to you. If you select three or five, that is also fine. The important thing is that you write down what you want to change.

2. When should you start to change? Make the decision with your intuition.

3. When will it be ready? When is the right time for you? Guide yourself using your intuition.

4. Plan in your calendar and make sure that the change happens.

What do you need to do to transform the negative victim mentality into something positive? If you look at the people who have success anywhere in the world, it is often people whose lives have been faced with challenges. Maybe they have been depressed, lost someone they loved, or lost a lot of money. They have transformed their setbacks into a creative force.

Where are you now—what do you want to achieve? Derive things with your intuition; what is it that puts an end to your development? Are you, for example, afraid to speak in front of people? Where does this fear come from? My own fear of speaking in front of people came from when I was eleven years old. It was someone on my sports team that told me that I was not good enough, and I then got the feeling that it is not worth saying anything because I never am good enough. Intuitively, I feel that this is the situation that created my blockage. I have replaced the feeling, by affirming that I am a dignified man and that I am good enough, whatever I do. Derive and identify the underlying cause of your blockage. Work all the time with your intuitive ability, and do not let the rational mind take over. It is easy to reason, "Oh, no, it cannot be from that time in my childhood." It is your inner critic you face when you go through the process of creating more balance in your life. Your inner critic is all your paradigms which keep you in your old belief about yourself and your limitations. When you meet the internal critic, have the courage to continue and do not listen to it. Your inner critic automatically generates external criticism, all according to the law of attraction. The law of attraction says that you attract everything that you really believe is the truth about yourself, deep down in your soul. So if you do want to have good results but you feel that you are not worth anything, it is unfortunately this that you will attract. External criticism is simply a reflection of your inner critic.

EXERCISE 7.4: *The limitation tree*

1. Draw a tree upside down. At the top you can draw your current situation and at the bottom, on the top of the tree, draw where you want to be.

2. Draw branches upside down where you write what prevents you from doing what you want to do both inside and outside yourself. It may, for example, be "having difficulty saying no" or "have difficulty with close relationships."

3. Feel intuitively that it is right.

4. Derive and solve every limitation with the Soulbalance method.

5. When you have derived the underlying cause, you can unlock the soul blockage.

6. What do you need to do so that your soul will replace the negative habit patterns you have created?

This exercise will really help you to get free from negativity. Let us take an example. John has difficulty saying no to people he loves, so each year he goes with his wife to her parents for Christmas dinner. Deep inside he wishes not to go, but he says nothing to avoid hurting his wife. John derives the soul cause of this behavior and finds that it goes back to the age of five. He barely spent any time with his father, who always was absent. This created a feeling in him of not being loved and not good enough. He then submitted to an inferior role where he believed that if he was nice to everyone, he would be considered good enough. Now that John has found the underlying cause, he needs also to dissolve the mental and physical paradigms that govern his life today to get balance at all levels. John really loves his wife, but he believes that he must do it her way to be affirmed, which is not true. John decides to tell his wife that he has had enough of the humiliating family dinners. His wife first looks surprised at John, not because of his message, but for the courage he shows for the first time. She responds by thanking John that he found a good reason to say no to these dinners for the first time in twenty years. It turns out that his wife hates the dinners even more than John, but she went there just to show that she is grateful for what the parents have done for her. Thanks to this decision, John and his wife initiate a healing process. His wife must also solve the underlying cause of her self-abusive behavior, and that she also can do after the physical change. To remove the conditioning is to ease the handbrake in a car. Now you just need to have a goal that is truly worth the effort to fight for. Your internal engine has now found the force needed to achieve everything you want.

Clear goals

Have you ever thought about what you can really accomplish? The problem for many when setting a goal is that they do not realize their full capacity. They do not think they can achieve things, because negative thoughts, emotions, and soul conditioning always make them give up without actually have tried. In order to achieve internal balance and external success, it is important to set a goal that you really want to achieve. Not any goal, but one that you know with your whole being: This I would like to achieve. Dream freely and rely on the intuitive thoughts that come up. Intuition is the tool the soul has given you to be able to access your full capacity. When you then start working towards your dreams and goals, you need to keep your intuition open that your dreams are possible, because when you begin and start to execute what you want to achieve, your conditioning will make itself heard. If you trust the negativity you then meet, there is no chance that you will succeed with what you dream about. Here it is important to dare to go straight through the old familiar thoughts and emotions that limit you. The paradigm does not recognize the dream and wants to get rid of it as soon as possible. If you have an action plan that you pursue towards your goals, you will sooner or later achieve your dreams, whatever the conditioning says. If you experience vibrations of dreams and opportunities, it is the soul's way of telling you that this is possible, whether you or others have a different view. If you do not see and feel the same thing, it is your conditioning, usually from childhood, which is making itself heard. Does the soul say that you can, but the paradigm says you cannot? If so, a conflict is occurring within you which the conditioning usually wins. The essential thing here is to rely on your intuition and go for your dreams.

Intuition often comes to you as an inner feeling, a feeling that you just know, but some people see images or get in touch with their intuition another way. When you work with your intuition, you will know deep inside when something is right. A heavy negative thought or feeling is always your paradigm talking. If you get a variety of negative conditioned thoughts in your mind, saying you are not good enough, you cannot, it is the soul saying that these fears must be considered, processed, and resolved to unlock your full potential. Here it is important to let the negative feelings arise to the surface, so you can free yourself from their negative force that is challenging your soul. When a feeling comes to the surface, you can resolve its negative force with the Soulbalance method, so you can achieve your goals. The big mistake many make is that they ignore the dreams and fears that the soul is trying to make them aware of, and then they live totally against the soul's ability to help them evolve in life. You might think it is unfair that some people easily reach success in life. But every soul has different challenges and needs to be challenged with different things in order to achieve the wholeness it needs in order to heal. The key is not how easy it is. The one who goes through more pain can create even more balance. Think of it as a process in which you heal yourself. Consider what you can learn from each critical situation in life, negative as well as positive. Often you will see the value of the lesson only when the pain has disappeared. Then you get an insight into how to use the experience. All external resistance is an indication of what you need to realize to heal the soul. Daring to meet your greatest fears is like balm for the soul. The soul yearns for that so you can grow and become the best you can be.

Paradigm for Success

Why do we have to struggle so to get over the negative we carry with us? Why can we not just begin to create success with our thoughts here and now? This is a very interesting topic. Imagine that your subconscious mind is like a glass of water that stores all the feelings that you experienced, whether they are positive or negative. You have filled your glass since childhood with negative or positive emotions, depending on what you experienced during your journey in life. Your subconscious also sucked up what emotions your parents carried on. Do you come from a background where everyone was secure in themselves and had good finances? The chances are greater that you quite effortlessly can create the same conditions. Unfortunately, most of us come from completely different circumstances, and the water glass is filled with poor self-esteem and poor finances. Many are trying to create success by filling the glass with positive things, but the glass is already full. To achieve your goals you have to replace the full glass with new, pure, fresh water that will help you solve the underlying cause which is stored on the soul level, and then change your habits and thoughts and your way of looking at money, health, and relationships. The soul conditioning one can solve directly with the Soulbalance method, but each habitual pattern of behavior may take up to three weeks to break, and the change takes the time it takes depending on what you carry around. A good way to change your habits and thoughts is to look for the opposite for your situation and learn to feel comfortable there. Once you have solved the soul cause of the soul as to why you felt uncomfortable in the new situation, you can become comfortable in the situation, and then you have changed your conditioning so that you can achieve the goals you have set.

Say, for example, you want to move to a bigger house in an area you previously only dreamed of. Right now, you stay as a third-generation resident in an area where financial conditions are tough. The solution is to stay more and more in your dream area, where you go house hunting, look at schools for the children, buy food there, and so on. You solve the underlying cause in the soul of why you feel so uncomfortable, and after a while you are so comfortable in the new area that you do not want to go back to the old. You have now created a new, positive conditioning and are ready for success, and therefore you have distanced yourself from what you do not want. If you just sit still where you are now, your subconscious does not know that you want a change, and hence it will remain absent.

The paradigm is always looking for the least possible resistance, making it much harder to break a paradigm than keep it. Here come eleven points that can help you develop and leave your conditioned life behind and become the best you can be. These points are there to help you really dare to take the leap and live your life fully using your intuition.

1. If you do not feel worthy of the change, it means that your paradigm says that what you want to change and achieve is not possible, neither in your or someone else's eyes. The solution is to dare to break the conditioning of indignity. This you can do by using five steps: a) You do not *try to* make the change but you *decide* to do it. b) You do not let anyone or anything stop you. c) You see it as your life's greatest challenge to change. d) You make sure that the goal is much larger than what you leave behind, that the goal has a greater spiritual value for you in your relationship with God. e) You make sure that what you really want to achieve gives you what you want in life. It does not always mean that something has to be bigger or better in the classical sense, because that often involves doing things to prove to others and one's conditioning that one is good enough. No, do what is right for you so that you know that you are following your divine path.

2. Perhaps the biggest reason why we do not change is that we do not know how to go about it. You do not have to know how it is going to happen, but just know that it will happen. With this decision, God will support you at just the right moment when change shall happen. This does not mean you disregard your action plans, but you do what you can and then leave the rest to God, who will make it happen. You will get the information you need while you relax with the belief that it will happen. You never know when you will get the divine support, but you know intuitively that it will happen. An inner, much larger trust in God has been created, and you can begin to enjoy the divine fruits.

3. Do not try to make change for someone else's sake. It is not a good idea. Each individual has his or her unique divine gifts, so to change to gain acceptance from someone else is not changing for the right reason. Do not take the big leap to be good enough for others, but to be true to yourself and become one with God.

4. "What would people say if I failed?" Many do not dare to pursue their dream due to the fear of failure. But if you are living your life with fear of failure as a yardstick, you will not reach far, because this fear is paralyzing. It is paralyzing not only to your creative ability, but also for your ability to really "ace" what you do, which really encourages you to take that extra step which distinguishes success from failure–not external superficial success, but the success that puts you in a winning position that is far larger than what your mind can understand. It is a rare luxury to enjoy the intuitive ability to create what you want when you want, but anyone can develop it. Dare to take the chance now to achieve this state, where everything really is possible.

5. "What if I do not get what I really want out of it?" That you cannot know until you really have tried. Many are the individuals who have waited their whole life to get the answer whether they really made the right choice. It is precisely the point: you do not know what the answer will be, but you try and create what you think is right for the moment. In retrospect, if you had the answers in advance you would have done things a little differently, but the focus is not on regrets but on your ability to solve challenges during the voyage. The more you can develop

this ability, the more you will grow, and the more you grow, the more you will develop this ability.

6. "Is there really any idea to do it?" Very many of us are stuck in thought patterns that hold us tolerably alive, thinking ourselves to be the worst we can be to maybe being good enough to be worthy to exist. The soul is always looking for new challenges. If you lower yourself to a mediocre level—based on what you, not on what others think—life will then often be dark, lonely, and empty, regardless of your so-called external success or having plenty of people around you.

7. The road to success is really the success. Once you reach a goal, it is only the external manifestation of the greatness you carry within you. Once you have decided to execute your dream, the success is a reality long before it reached the physical form.

8. Worry less, do more. To constantly worry about what will happen does not solve anything. My advice to you is to go out in life with the inner realization that everything will be fine, even if the journey can be bumpy. Saying that it will be fine does not mean you will live a fairy-tale life as you read about in books, but you will get to what you need to be able to use your full soul capacity.

9. Imagine that what you want to achieve is achievable. Always start from the view that whatever comes to you and can help you to grow is exactly what you need. It is so easy to belittle the divine messages

because they might not come in the form and packaging you would expect. But what you expect, you can already achieve.

10. The unpredictable is the real gift in life. I am talking about everything that science cannot prove—being able to laugh in a heartfelt and spontaneous way, to feel happy when you see a child play, or anything else that may seem trivial to others but brings joy to your life whatever it is. The more you can feel the joy of the present and be part of that a little bit, the less inclined you will be trying to create something to be good enough for others.

11. How about dying with a smile on your lips? Imagine that you live a life where you finally get to die with a smile on your lips, instead of having your face marked by pain and sorrow that life never came with what you wanted. You are the creator of your life, so you can decide what to do with your life. You cannot always influence what is happening, but you can always influence how you perceive what is happening.

To dare to make Decisions

So many of us are so conditioned by what others want us to do that we have completely lost the power to make our own decisions. Thousands of years ago we could not live without our intuition, as it often saved us from attacks from animals or other people. There was no time to call an authority or doctor to get answers to everything, because by then you were already dead. We still have this enormous capacity, which is a gift from God; but we do nothing with it. When we are not using our full capacity, it creates a kind of internal frustration that can come to the surface in the form of various symptoms to make us aware that not everything is fine. It can be anything from burnout to indifference, but what the symptoms have in common is that your inner self is not satisfied with what is happening in your life. In many cases it feels comfortable not to make a decision, but it is devastating for our own creative power. Now take back your inner power! Be a decision maker to be reckoned with, and both you and your surroundings will grow from this. In the beginning, it can be frustrating and you may feel uncertain, but use the frustration to grow as a person. Frustration is, in many respects, a catalyst needed for you to begin to act at all. Unfortunately, many misinterpret the frustration and use it as a driving force for negative things, such as criminal acts or self-destructive behavior, including alcohol and drug abuse. What the soul would like to say by using frustration is that it wants change, which means that you should take charge of your life and live your life according to your inner truth. It goes wrong when the frustration is not seen as a way to grow but as fuel for destructive behavior. It is your and my personal responsibility to ensure that this does not happen. For some, it has gone so far that they have no ability to se this insight, and then they need external help to solve the trauma because they do not respond normally to frustration. This may be helped by the Soulbalance method, which helps individuals to resolve their trauma once and for all.

Do you find it hard to make decisions? You must practice and dare to make them. There are two ways to do this:

1. You make the decision based on how it will work in the long run. Ask yourself: Is this good for me long term? The point is that you circumvent the passivity that many of us have been conditioned with and which keeps us in a sometimes convenient, but always devastating state. Make the decision regardless of what your paradigm says and you will eventually get rid of just that paradigm when you solve the underlying cause.

2. Make decisions based on what you want, not what your fears and conditioning say. It may be that you dare to buy a house even if you do not think you are worth it, or that you dare to ask another person to dance even though you can be rejected.

The more you dare to do this, the more you become a decision-maker, and, of course, the more you become a decision-maker, the better access you get to your intuitive ability.

Chapter 8

The Universe is with You

We have moved from an agricultural society to an industrial society on to an IT society. Religion is becoming less and less important in society, but the interest in personal and spiritual development is increasing. We have now entered what we call the conscious society. In the conscious society, we aim at all times to create more balance in the soul, more awareness of how we live. If we could agree that we have a mutual creation energy and a mutual God, it is then irrelevant who we are and where we come from. Then people would not fight; we would not have religious wars. Everything must have meaning, and the meaning must be from somewhere. I claim that it comes from God, who is the energy behind the creation. God is not tied to any religion but is a clean energy source. All wars in progress are linked to power and/or religion. It is time for us individuals to regain power, so that we can avoid all these conflicts and wars. The individual has the link to the universe and does not need to be good enough for a religion. As we in Sweden have begun to leave the church, many people believe that we are less spiritual. I argue the opposite—that people are more spiritual, but they cannot be members of an institution that says we must be a certain way to be good enough. It must be people's choice how they want to handle their relationship with God. More and more people are interested in developing their spirituality and being one with God. This is not just available for the small number of the so-called enlightened; everyone has the opportunity, even if there are some who argue the opposite.

No human wants to be restrained, but religion has been used for millennia for that particular task, to suppress people. The time has come for every individual to do what everyone wants with his or her life. It would be rather odd if we only were good enough for God if we belonged to a particular religion. Even stranger would be to argue that one religion is more important than another. It is now time for everyone to live next to each other no matter what religion you belong or do not belong to. Religions fights for God, who exists within all of us all the time. It is the soul that deep inside is connected to God outside us. It means that we all can have this relationship with God, all the time. We need not go to church, the mosque, or the synagogue if we do not want to. It is not wrong to do so, but you do not have to. You are good enough in God's eyes all the time. Since everything and everyone comes from the same creation energy, we really always hurt ourselves if we hurt others. This applies not only to mankind, but also to all animals and plants. We humans have decided that we are the most important thing on earth, but who has really given us this right? It is not God anyway, for in the eyes of God we are all equal: plants, animals, and humans. It does not mean that it is wrong for all humans, for example, to eat meat or to cut a tree, but the value of all living things is the same. This applies, of course, to all people, regardless of whether they are homeless or the richest in the world. Creating success in harmony with God and the universe is about so much more than looking down at those who are not good enough according to society's norms. It is mainly about all of us being able to live out our inner truth, which is our connection to God. Without the meaning of life, humanity dies. So far, the meaning for many has been to win at the expense of others. But now the time has come when we can make profits within ourselves and simultaneously help others. A goal that is set in line with our inner truth always serves both the individual and humanity. With a world filled with true individuals, there is no room for hatred, wars, and conflicts. These exist only as long as we do not have the individual and collective awareness to solve them. They are the collective, external, physical symptoms, just as we have individual challenges. Imagine if the world's leaders would make decisions according to the Soulbalance method. We know that they would not get intuitive responses that hurt others. Right now many decisions are made based on ego, which is conditioned by the power that passed through generations of oppression and suffering. Intuition is the messenger of God, who also ensures collective healing.

Closer to God

Science argues that God does not exist for God's existence cannot be proven. But even spirituality, love, and feelings are yet to be proven, and still they exist. Remove the burden of proof from God. It is sufficient enough that we know that there must be an intelligence behind everything. Science often tries to ridicule those who have a belief in God. It is actually thanks to God that we have science. Science has just reached the consciousness that God allows. Man has been endowed with the divine ability to make the impossible possible and thereby be co-creator with God. But without God, the thought would not even exist. I grew up in an atheist home. I did not care about God as the subject was so influenced by religion. Then you had to believe in Christianity, Judaism, or Islam. But when I started working with intuition, I discovered what God really was. I discovered that God for me not was an old man, but more an energy. The energy comes from the origin of the creation. It took energy to create the entire universe, and God is the energy behind the creation. Then, God's energy created the earth, man, animals, the universe, and all universes. We are part of the creation energy, and that means that when we believe in ourselves, we believe in the energy that lies within us. It is the same energy going all the way back to the creation of the universe. The soul is a reflection of all that you are just now, but also a reflection of everything from today back to the moment when you started to exist and got a soul. The soul carries its lessons to be learned to the next life, so examine yourself, find your challenges, and make the best you can from this life. See your soul as a database with a series of memories from this life and, in some cases, from past lives and the creation energy. The creation energy was a time when everything was just energy and no physical existence was there. Some people have blockages from this time, which takes its expression in purely existential questions. When life does not flow as it should, it is often suppressed in the soul database with a negative paradigm we must become aware of and solve. You can intuitively derive the underlying or soul cause and, with the help of God, heal the wound in the soul. God wants to say: Do you want to be completely free and one with God? Do not follow others; stop follow rites, stop believing that you have to do things in a special way to be good enough. The most important thing is to be true to yourself, no matter what other people say and your paradigm says. The enlightenment for you is within you, here and now, and not with someone else. To almost manically follow rituals to make contact with God is far from God's desire. We are all selected as individuals and as a whole. It is our responsibility as individuals and as a whole to make the best of life here on earth.

Closer to God:

• You can never buy your way closer to God. This means that no money or positions of power in the world can make you closer to God. The simplest, most unknown person may have a much stronger relationship with God than a so-called spiritual leader.

• You can never give alms or gifts to be closer God. Give because you want, but do not consider that you are a better person for that sake. You can give in so many ways, and the physical gift is just one of many ways to help others. If you give only to strengthen your ego, it is not the way to go. Gifts must come from the heart for you to get the soul satisfaction you are looking for.

• No one else can get you closer to God. Your connection to God is a direct connection between you and God's energy. No religion is needed in this contact, but it can be applied if the need is there.

• God is really indifferent to worship. It is enough to be true to yourself to get the contact you want with God. If you are true to yourself, you are also indirectly true to God, since you originally have been created by the divine creation energy.

Anxiety and belief in God

Have you ever had severe anxiety? In Sweden we call it *ångest*. Can you imagine a more loaded word? No other language can describe the agony in the same powerful way. You almost feel the pain by simply pronouncing the word. Why is this fascination with the word ångest (anxiety) so popular? Is it that we Swedes feel worse than any other people? Actually there is no reason for this, except that we have a very strong Lutheran conditioning in Sweden which more or less says that we should not be happy, but that we should suffer to be good enough for God, in a society where the belief in God as a whole is almost eliminated. Clearly, this creates existential anguish for many. It is not that I advocate a retreat to a society that is greatly influenced by Christianity. But how do we fill the vast emptiness that many of us feel without linking it to Christianity or any other religion? As long as we live in a society where we want individuals to make ethical decisions in accordance with laws based on Christian fundamentals, but we do not have contact with God overall, there will be a strong spiritual yearning among many people, which manifests itself in anxiety. This is not a matter of fear over whether to buy a pair of trousers or not, but the existential anguish which makes many people feel that they do not have any value being here on earth at all. Through the years, many people have found comfort in the traditional religions' answers to questions regarding the meaning of life and the existential life issues. But now we want more and more individual freedom, while we want to feel a greater spirituality. How does this go together?

We have reached a point in time where it is time to dissolve the existential anxiety that so many of us carry with us. There is a solution, and it is to dare to be the best you can without all the dogmas that you have learned that you traditionally have to follow to be good enough. In God's eyes we all are good enough regardless of color, race, religion, sex, and so on. The time has come when every individual must fully realize that we all have the same basic worth. This is easy to say, but they are empty words in both Sweden and other countries. We must recognize this fact, not on a superficial level, but on a deep existential plane where everything and everyone really has the same value. How will this happen? First, many of us would feel good to recognize that there is a God, whether we believe in the traditional God or not. The book's purpose is not to sell you a particular belief in God, but only to use the opportunity to try to understand that there may be another dimension than what is taught in our secular society, where the internal ethics and morality have vanished. All was not better in the old days, but we had at least the Ten Commandments as a guide. Everyone did not, of course, live following the Ten Commandments, but we had some type of joint, inner ethical guideline. Today we lack these common values, which means that many are struggling with their inner morality and faith. The problem with modern law is that it has the Ten Commandments as a base, but we no longer believe in God. We have as society lost the individual ethical guidelines that were present in our religious faith. Actually, we can all re-create this guide. It is within us at all times. With the help of our intuition, we know what is right or wrong. Pure intuition, free from conditioning, helps you be true to yourself, and with that you follow the ethical framework which is your intuitive contact between you and God. I myself have noticed that God only lets me make intuitive decisions that follow the divine law that we all have access to. If I break this unwritten contract, I do not have access to the intuition anymore. Obviously this divine contact even works for so-called atheists, because God condemns no one, regardless of faith or lack of faith. What we are talking about is not any religion but about God as an energy, and then there is generally a greater acceptance of God. Everyone believes in something, and I have realized that if we choose to believe in something bigger than ourselves, in this case God, divine healing can always take place. God does not care about any hierarchies, but is cleansing and healing for those who want help. Today much legislation goes against what is right for the individual, so all yearn for an additional ethical guideline where we can get the answers to what society does not have answers to. It can be questions such as, "Am I good enough as a person?" or "What is my role here on earth?" Anyone can search and find answers to this if he or she is ready to create a personal contact and establish a personal guidance with God.

In order to overcome this internal ethical struggle that so many of us perceive, we have a choice between two options:

1. To totally deny God's existence and just continue as we are with a society where we do not have any inner ethical guidelines to follow, with a huge existential anxiety as a result.

2. To affirm God's existence from a nonreligious perspective in a society where religious belonging does not matter, where it does not even play

any role if you are defined as an atheist or not. What matters is that we are seeking contact with our internal guideline that can actually give us answers to what is right and wrong. This inner guideline is God's gift to us through the universal soul.

You can ask questions about yourself and your existence with the help of your intuition and get the answers you need. At first, I almost only got yes and no answers, when I was very skeptical and was only open for an analytical approach that relied on black or white, yes or no, right or wrong, now or tomorrow. Eventually I discovered that God allows us to communicate quite freely with the universal soul and gives us answers about what we want and need. What is so amazing about establishing a personal internal ethical guide is that you never have to go through the existential crisis questioning whether you are or are not good enough. How is this possible? Ask yourself these four questions and you are on your way: a) What do I want to do with my life? b) What is it that makes me really get the existential satisfaction that I seek? c) How can I connect my individual will and goals into a larger perspective, where others in the world benefit? d) Who am I damaging by living the life I live today? If we would all ask ourselves these individual questions, we would not only take personal responsibility, but we would take the collective responsibility the whole world is waiting for but which cannot be imposed by laws and regulations. It can never be society's responsibility to ensure that we do this, but it is our individual responsibility. If both you and I and everyone else would take our individual responsibilities, all causes of war, repression, and denial of self-value would disappear.

This may take a while to execute, but it is entirely possible. God is always with you, whether you believe it or not.

Why is there so much evil and misery if God exists? This is a common question when spirituality and religion are discussed. God does not determine how we live; God lives out his energy and vision with the people who choose the positive path. God can not physically self-create the miracles you and I perform, but they come through an individual and a collective responsibility towards God. By thinking positively and being true to ourselves, we will directly and indirectly go the right way. However, if we choose the ego road where we live only for our own benefit, God will not support our choice, and the imbalance that results is a fact. There is always a struggle within each individual between being true to themselves and God on one hand, and society at large on the other hand. When we as individuals and society have got enough wisdom about how we all should live in balance and harmony, we will have a peaceful and healthy world. Until that day we can only trust that God supports each individual to never violate himself or herself, or someone else. To take advantage of others never gets us closer to God, but provides only temporary satisfaction for those who violate others. By observing each violation and then doing something positive to resolve it, we go against a more and more enlightened society. God is pure and has not entered into a special relationship with a selected ethnic group or religion. In the eyes of God, all are equal, and that value should be respected around the world. When humanity collectively realizes this, we will have world peace and a world free from violations.

Where we will then take humanity is another matter. Once we have achieved a certain goal, the motivation decreases. Therefore, we constantly need to find new challenges for ourselves in order to contribute to a better world. God is behind a world in balance, and God needs help to create just that. The question is what the next step should be for you, me, and humanity.

Is it my Ego or my Soul that speaks?

What does the ego want and what does the soul want? The ego is thinking about what is best for you short term, but the soul always thinks of the long-term balance. To be driven by the ego may be to avoid a particular situation not to be confronted with a negative feeling. The soul says, however: Go through fear so you can reach internal balance. The ego can also make you make money short term to show others how good you are, while the soul creates good finances to achieve long-term freedom for you and your family. For an outsider, both options can seem exactly alike, but you know to which category you belong. The challenge is to dare to say no to the egos whims and instead rely on the soul's response. Those answers will come when you develop your intuitive abilities, and this is the only way to go if you want to be free of the ego's manipulation. The intuition is completely neutral and sees you for who you really are. Intuition is God, who communicates to and through you. You may not always be satisfied with the intuitive solution short term, but long term it is always right. Remember that you never have to put yourself down because of others' opinions and accusations. Your soul has, when it is in balance, its own ethical system. For example, if someone says that you are wrong, but what you are doing feels intuitively right, follow your intuition, no matter what external resistance and opinions you meet. Sometimes the inner spiritual justice system is out of order and you may then perform the most horrendous acts, as the enormous violations of others that we can read in the headlines.

If you do unethical things:

1. Learn how to derive with the Soulbalance method why you perform unethical acts. It is not really you who wants to do the negative, but your conditioning has taken over your internal justice system. If you would like to solve this, it is possible.

2. Only you can decide if you are healed or not. You need develop your intuition as far as you can, to know if you are right or wrong.

3. Please note that we do carry the harm that we consciously cause with us to the next life and we must be accountable for that then.

4. God forgives you, but it does not make what you did wrong, right. You must bear the consequences of your actions to yourself and God.

5. Repeat steps 1-4 if necessary.

Dare to release the control and let God in

There is so much we try to control here in life. It can be everything from the perfect birth to being perfect at work. Sooner or later you will notice that it is irrelevant how much you control, because things are still not always the way you had in mind. Then you need to dare to let go and really have faith in the process that we cannot control. For many, it is very difficult, because control is often synonymous with success. But the real success is when you create an unlimited trust in that which is much larger than yourself, in God. God is not a magician who does what you think is best, but we are all part of a giant puzzle where every piece has something to add. It is through your own discoveries that you test your piece of the puzzle at different places, and often you will find the right place for it. It is not until you let go and trust that your piece of the puzzle has a place that the whole puzzle is completed, both individually and collectively. If we knew exactly how this process happens, then there would be no innovation, no meaning, and everything would be monotonous, year after year. When you invest 100 percent in life or work, everything will fall into place. A seemingly meaningless life can be transformed into a life with meaning when you are one with God. So many have tried to explain how this happens, but actually God is with you all the time;, you just have to become aware of it and allow the flow in and with you. When you do this, no person or thing can stop you, for you do not any longer do things to be good enough, but for a higher purpose. When you do something for a larger cause, the ego releases its grip on you and you become all calm inside. Imagine being free of the burden of trying to be good enough for others, with all that means. When we dare to live as a part of the flow, we do not allow others' limiting thoughts and comments to determine where we end up in life; instead we end up where we want without fear of failure, or fear of failure will sooner or later show up if you do things for the wrong reason. Do things for the right reason and you will have the power to continue, no matter how tough it seems.

Chapter 9

To Grow as a Person

When a child does not receive any encouragement to grow, he or she does not want to grow and develop. Children think that when they do not develop, then they are good enough for the parents. I never received any encouragement from my parents, so the more I did to develop and create success, the worse I felt. This has become the theme of my life: whatever I do, I am not good enough because I do not get any appreciation for it. I have all the time tried to do things to get my parents' praise, but have never got it. The reason that neither of them had the power to give me appreciation and encouragement is likely that neither of them got any when they grew up. If you are a parent, always encourage your child! It may be for schoolwork, a sports performance, that the child is a good companion. If the parents do not give any encouragement, they indirectly say that the child is not good enough. And if the child feels that he or she is not good enough, he or she usually also feels that life is not worth anything. If you did not receive appreciation from your parents, it does not matter how successful you are on the external front. You can be rich, have a fancy job, and enjoy a great social life. It does not help. You can never grow and develop more than your parents' unconscious and conscious constraints allow you without consciously changing direction as an adult. This means that all negative baggage they carry with them becomes part of you whether you like it or not. Imagine a computer that is full of viruses and spyware. You take it over from your parents and then give it later to your own children. It is not until the children make active choices as adults that these negative programs can be removed. So many of us parents carry around things that we are not satisfied with, such as poor self-esteem, unhealthy attitudes about money, or a lack of faith in true love. Instead of consciously changing the way we look at a situation, as we can do as adults, we let it just stay there, expecting it to change on its own. Perhaps within ourselves, but especially for our children, we need to distance ourselves from what does not work for us. We need to see our upbringing without either idealizing or condemning it. If you do not look neutrally on your upbringing, regardless of how it was, you cannot get an honest picture of what has not worked.

EXERCISE 9.1: *Your dream becomes reality*

1. Write down how your current situation looks in terms of your finances, health, and relationships. Write down what the situation looks like in practical terms: how much money you have in the bank, how you really feel, and how your relationship is to yourself and others. Write as much detail as possible to get a confirmation of where you really stand in life.

2. If your question is regarding your child, write down how the child's situation looks in the same areas. Since your child is a reflection of you, you can usually see the reason for his or her results in yourself, even if they are deeply hidden and you do not want to recognize them for yourself. If the child, for example, is struggling with anorexia, take a look at what you or your partner have transferred from your conditioning to

the child's conditioning, with associated external negative results. You have now found the present cause for your situation.

3. Find out where you want to be with your life. Say you had a huge creative ability as a child but received no encouragement for it at all. You may then have started to do everything possible to push down your creative vein to make your parents happy, because that is how children react when they want to get love and confirmation. They shut down one talent after another until they are just like you want them to be, or, even worse, like you do not want them to be but as you unconsciously signal to them that they should be because of what you think about yourself deep inside. No secrets can be kept from children. You may be able to hide the visible, but the kids capture all imbalances through their unspoiled intuitive ability. They take part of all your worries and problems.

4. How would your life look if you had gotten the encouragement you really yearned for but did not get? Write your answers down in detail on a piece of paper, as a child would write down what he or she wishes for as a birthday gift or a Christmas present. Dream as much as you can and let go of any thoughts and impressions that are holding you back.

5. Write as if your dreams already have come true. Feel that the creative vein is opened up again. The more committed you become, the more you come in touch with your inner truth. This is, furthermore, an excellent exercise for your child, where you can inspire him or her to dream freely.

6. Now that you know where you stand with your conditioning, you also know where you want to be. Now figure out what it is inside or outside of you limiting your life. Make a list of internal factors and a list of external factors in all three areas (economy, health, relationships). The more detail you write and the deeper you dig, the easier it will be to create change.

7. Once you have made your list of limitations, it is time to take a look at each one of them. You may have written down ten or twelve limitations, maybe more, maybe less. Resolve every limitation by using the Soulbalance method. Is the underlying cause of the limitation in this life, in a past life, or in the creation energy? Circle the answer that you are drawn to intuitively. Find intuitively how old you were when the conditioning occurred (if it was in this life). What happened? Feel intuitively what happened. What emotions come to the surface when you find the cause? Trust your intuition and write down what comes to you.

8. Write an action plan of how to get where you want to be in life. You should now transform your limitations into opportunities. You have solved your limitations on the soul level, but you now need to manifest this through mental, emotional, and physical change. Even this is done with the help of your intuition, because your conditioning can create the wrong time frame, so you destroy everything you want indefinitely. If you do not make any changes, neither you nor your child's situation will improve.

9. Plan and break down the goal in years, months, weeks, and days. For each day write down three points that will take you closer to your goal, and then make sure you do them. Performing the three steps every day will make you break your bad habits if you make sure you do what you promised yourself. Relate to the intuitive decisions as above mentioned.

10. Here is an example of three daily issues that are related to you never have received any encouragement. Note that this is an example and may not be exactly what you should do:

- To treat yourself to a little present for your wonderful day.
- To write up that you love yourself twenty times.
- To call the company you want to work for, but had previously not dared to contact.

Symptoms and their Causes

Did you, as a child, get enough encouragement to grow and evolve as a human being? If you did not, you stagnate on the physical, mental, emotional, and soul level, and you develop a variety of symptoms. The symptoms are there to show that you are on the wrong road, too far away from your inner truth. All that the parents radiate—if they hate themselves, think that they are forever doomed to have bad finances or poor health, if they have racist values, and so forth—all is conditioned in the child. Because of this you cannot abuse alcohol and tell your children that they should not drink, or smoke and say that they should not smoke, or have poor finances and say that you should help them to get good finances. What the parents radiate conditions the child and creates the same pattern over and over again. This can be seen in many families where different family members, generation after generation, show symptoms for everything from poor finances to a low self-esteem. The next exercise will show that most individuals may exhibit a variety of symptoms that actually come from a few underlying causes. My symptoms have been numerous, ranging from allergies and phobias to depression and the desire to live no longer. I never really wanted to commit suicide; I just did not want to live. In my case the causes for my external negative symptoms basically came from two situations: 1) that I was thrown in a swimming pool by a swim instructor, with my parents' consent, to learn to swim when I was five years old and lived in England. I sank like a stone and from this developed enormous fear to trust anyone; 2) that a teacher in the English school threatened me that God would punish me so that I could die. This also happened when I was five years old. This created a variety of existential traumas with a deep depression as a result.

EXERCISE 9.2: *Many symptoms – few reasons*

1. You can have a variety of symptoms that can be traced back to the same underlying cause. Most people usually have two to four underlying causes related to their biggest problems. Start looking up symptom after symptom and see what traumas are causing most of your external symptoms. Derive and solve the traumas with the Soulbalance method. The underlying cause may come from several incidents on the same theme.

2. Once you find the underlying causes, you put in where you want to end up. Say you found that you felt you were not good enough because of something that happened when you were four years old. Write down on a piece of paper that you are good enough as a person. Use it as an affirmation and read it ten times morning and evening. Since it takes about three weeks to break a habit pattern, you need to repeat each affirmation for three weeks. Once you find incident after incident and affirm the opposite positive feeling to each one, the underlying cause will not have any power anymore and your symptoms will disappear.

3. In my case, I felt that I was not worth living after what happened with the teacher and the threat of the divine punishment. It took approximately to the age of fourteen years before the symptoms came to the surface. It is typical when you become a victim of something that the symptoms come up at a later date. Many childhood traumas makes their debut as symptoms between fourteen and twenty-five years of age. One underlying cause may create many negative external symptoms. When you correct the cause with the Soulbalance method, not only that symptom disappears, but all the symptoms that the underlying cause created. You get a kind of turbo power when you heal yourself from your external negative symptoms. In this way I became free of all my allergies and phobias within five weeks.

4. If you have not found the underlying cause in the soul, it will be as if your affirmation, such as "I love myself in every situation," bounces. It will never reach your soul, and no change can be made. But when you

find the underlying cause and create an affirmation that runs counter to the negative cause, what you want to happen actually can happen.

5. It is not enough to just repeat the affirmations; you also need to expose yourself to situations where you can develop your ability. To simply be in the bedroom with the blinds pulled down and repeat that you are worthy will not work. But if you expose yourself to situations where you have previously felt that you not good enough and quietly to yourself repeat the affirmation, you will finally feel worthy. It may be to speak in front of a group, shoot a penalty in soccer, or write an essay.

When I had healed myself and strived to become the best I could become and be one with my inner truth, lots of negative external symptoms, such as the hypersensitivity to food, electricity, perfume, and more, disappeared. What was as good or even better was that my children's allergies healed through my development. We are soul connected to our children regardless of whether they are our own children or adopted children, so when we grow, they grow. We have chosen each other to get the best opportunity to grow as people.

Break the negative Patterns and set Goals to Grow

You can break the negative patterns coming from not receiving what you needed from your parents, whether they are in terms of finances, health, or relationships. We will start with the finances: If you have poor finances, it has often to do with your childhood. Derive with the Soulbalance method and circle the point in time that it comes up. Go ahead and trace back; what happened then? You can do the same with your health problems. The reason for diseases often has an entirely different cause other than just what you see in the physical body. For example, obesity is often caused by soul blockages. If your soul conditioning tells you to be fat because you are not good enough, you will struggle in vain to be a normal weight and to maintain your normal weight until you do something about your soul blockage. You need to find the cause of your obesity. Maybe it is because you hate yourself because you were a victim of an assault as a child. Derive the answer with the Soulbalance method and find the underlying cause. When you get rid of your blockage, you can get and maintain the weight you want. If this does not resolve the matter directly, it does not mean that you have not found the right place. There may be more blockages that impact this state. To grow as a person takes a lot of daring. When you are in a situation where you have the chance to create the life you want, most people do not dare to change. They suffer a paralyzing fear of failure. Then it takes guts to climb out of your comfort zone. Where you are now may be comfortable, but without challenges you can become depressed and stop developing. When you set up goals for yourself, forcing yourself out of your comfort zone, you can get symptoms such as nervousness and anxiety. But if you just relax and change your life in the direction of your destination, these symptoms will disappear.

To set goals to grow as a person is extremely important. When you set up goals for yourself, you should ask yourself two questions: 1) How do I restrict myself? 2) How can I achieve my inner truth? To set goals is a powerful way to get out of a deadlock in life. When you are stuck, it is easy to give up and say that there is not anything you can do. You can feel like a victim. Then you need to start the process to actually create something. The process starts by setting goals and establishing an action plan to reach your goals. When you write up your goals and your plan, every part of you will react. Then, trust the intuitive feeling you get; otherwise the risk is that you let your conditioning limit you. Your conditioning will always try to steer you back to your old patterns. It is important that you have confidence in yourself. No one else can know what is best for you except yourself. Have you done what feels right for you? Then you have nothing to regret, even if you do not succeed with every project. It is also important to have confidence to the whole. Even when you trust yourself 100 percent, you need to get energy from the outside. In religions it is called the prayer. Trust that when you actually create something, there is a power greater than yourself who supports you in this. When you create something that is good not only for yourself but for the whole, this power opens up and supports you.

The important detoxification

When you feel bad, it is frequently one of two possible reasons. One is that you are going down, that you get filled with a lot of negative energy. Or it could be the opposite—that you are cleaning out soul clutter. Then it is positive and the soul is connected. You just need to find out what kind of trauma to clean out. When you know it, you only need to accept the feelings involved. The feeling might be similar to when you take in negative energy, but the difference is that the cleansing is a healing process. How can you tell the difference between these two? When you heal, you will feel deep inside your soul that you are about to clean out. In the pain you know that something is positive. When it is pitch dark, then the negative paradigm is on its way in. The more you try to keep a negative feeling or thought under control, the more it will control your life from your subconscious mind. The solution is: Find the feeling, let it come to the surface, release it, and replace it with a new thought or feeling that is positive. Negative energy can flow in two directions: into you and out from you. So long as you remain conditioned by others, it flows into you, but when you are prepared to confront the negativity, it flows out of you. The problem is that the feeling you experience is exactly the same when you heal the problem as when it comes into you. Therefore you need to know intuitively what process you are in. Ask yourself the question and identify the correct answer: "Is it negative conditioning on its way in, or am I cleansing out an old paradigm?"

EXERCISE 9.3: *Is your feeling in a healing or a conditioning stage?*
1. We are feeling all the negative emotions in our lives. Either you build up more negative feelings within yourself, or you heal the old feelings that were locked. The feeling you experience is often the same in both directions. Practice now to intuitively feel what process you are in:

• The feeling is about to go in (you are building up more negativity within you). This occurs when something happens that is negative, for example, when you suffer emotional abuse, or as long as you live under conditioning which is caused by negative events during your childhood or in past lives.

• The feeling is on the way out in your healing process. You are now in a process where you try to heal the trauma that it is locked in your soul.

You can, with the help of the Soulbalance method, identify the cause of the trauma and become free from the devastating feeling that is locked in your soul.

2. Circle the option for that particular situation or feeling you think of. Your intuitive power will guide you to choose what is right for you. Let go of the conditioned thought and rely on the sensation that comes to you. If you get an alternative one, you need to look over your life and make the external changes. If you get option two, you need to find out the underlying cause using the Soulbalance method.

When I needed to do something that was important for me and my family, negative things happened. I injured my eye so that I could hardly see, and I got a paralysing cold. It was my old conditioning trying to get me to stay in my old patterns. Intuitively I knew that I would continue on, and when I went through the fear and continued with what I should do, the cold and the problem of the eye disappeared. In this way I could implement what I planned to do. This was a symptom of the healing process. I could have had the same symptoms in a different situation, when the damaged eye alone would have been something destructive which had nothing to give to me. Often people who are moving into an acute crisis are not aware of their intuition, and my job is to help my clients to go from the harmful mode to a healing mode when the time is right. Having to wait for forty years to heal, as happened in my case, should not be necessary for anyone.

Identify the Resistance

When you do not get the results you want in life, this is usually because you are sending yourself subconscious messages saying that you are not good enough. Many of these messages come from childhood, before the age of seven. Before the age of seven we do not have a conscious ability to accept or reject the messages we get, so all messages are automatically entered in our subconscious mind. Then, they are there and govern our lives. To stop the messages, you must identify your inner truth and seek it regardless of external circumstances. Identify the resistance and release the energy that the resistance has locked in the soul. The solution is to learn to rely on your intuition and free yourself from the negative conditioning using your intuition and healing yourself according to the Soulbalance method. I use this approach with my intuition with everything I do in my life. For example, if I am at the doctor's and get asked if I want to implement a treatment, or if I have to choose between two schools for my children. I feel intuitively what feels right and make the decision after that. It is always right. Look for the vibration that is beyond the gut feeling, at a higher frequency. Then we have to rely on it. When we jump back and forth between the gut feeling, intuition, and science, it easily becomes wrong. I argue that the more you go into creating life with the help of your intuition, the better it gets.

What happens when we go through a change, when we take ourselves to the point where we want to be with the help of intuition, is that old conditioning comes up to the surface as fear. Often we get stopped by these fears when we are trying to achieve what we really want. Then we need to make an action plan and set goals, which takes us right through the fears. If we defeat the fears, we are growing, and we can create a better life for ourselves and others. Basically there are two fears that destroy our way to success more than any other: the fear of failure, and the fear of success. If you are afraid to fail, you do not try, and the fear of success holds you back. If you let these emotions steer you all the time, you will not achieve balance in life. Look at the fear of success, derive the underlying cause of the feeling, and see if you have any blockages. Do the same with the fear of failure.

Take advantage of your Freedom

Freedom is doing what you want, when you want, with whoever you want. In Sweden we have the right under the law, yet it is a minority who use this 100 percent. Why is this so? If we have the freedom to create what we want, but we do not, it must be due to an inner prison. This means that we limit our thoughts and dreams to being good enough. It depends a lot on the "Jante (mediocre) Law" that you are not allowed to be better then anyone else, which is huge in Sweden, keeping us stuck in mediocrity. The law says that we must not stick out and be the best we can be. This law is not official, but it guides us as much as if it were a law that was real and must be followed. When we do not follow common laws, we can get punished and even end up in jail. But the "Jante Law," which we in fact may break whenever we want, we follow in detail even without any police or other authorities needing to reprimand us. We are stuck in this mental, invisible prison which destroys all dreams and opportunities without anyone mentioning what we have done wrong. Is it not the time to recognize that this lack of liberty in many ways is as serious as being stuck in a real prison? The question is where you are in your life in relation to where you want to be. If it is your internal "Jante" that holds you back, or if it is the external, it is high time to do something about it. Look around and see all the bitter, disappointed faces. In newborns or with small children, you will not see these faces; they are created by decades of self-loathing and failure. Failure according to whom? Not that we are really failures, but we often feel unsuccessful when we do not live up to society's or others' standards for how we should be to be good enough. Most of us are struggling with exactly the same thoughts, so to try to be good enough for someone else, who does not even know if he or she is good enough, is both meaningless and negative.

Would it not be much better if each individual developed his or her own ability to confirm himself or herself, so that we do not for the rest of our lives remain dependent on this drug, which often indirectly or directly kills us? The key is to realize that you really do not need to be good enough for others to be good enough. The realization is not directly through advice from others, but it comes when you deep inside the soul understand that this is a truth for you. When the soul knows this truth, nobody can take that away from you, as this truth is much more powerful than anything else you see and experience. If you do not know this truth, then there is nothing wrong with you, but it is your conditioning sending you fake images that you are not good enough. When you realize that your conditioning is your conditioning and nothing else, you can get the perspective on life you need to heal. Life is a gift from God, and our gift to God is to do the best with it. If we really understood this at a deeper level, there would not be so many people running around feeling sorry for themselves. Unfortunately self-pity enhances just what you believe about yourself. What do you need to do to move on if you feel sorry for yourself? Realize first that your self-pity is not your true self. You do not actually have self-pity, but your conditioning says you do. Since your self-pity is not an absolute truth, there is no point to believe in it. But paradigms are usually so strong that they make you completely assured that you are not good enough. But in God's eyes, you are always good enough; otherwise you would not have come to this earth.

Here I have created a special exercise regarding self-pity, as self-pity locks so much negative energy in the soul. To transform "I cannot, must not, not good enough" to "I can, I am allowed to, and I am good enough" is essential for lasting success.

EXERCISE 9.4: *To transform self-pity to success*
If you now are struggling with self-pity, you need to derive and solve the underlying cause of your conditioning:

1. What is the outer symptom of your self-pity?

2. Does the symptom come from this life, past lives, or from the creation energy? Circle what you are intuitively drawn to.

3. Trace back to the time when the cause was created if it is in this life. Circle the age that you are drawn to. (For previous lives and the creation energy, this is not necessary.)

4. What happened? Write down what intuitively comes to you. If it is difficult to find a trauma, write down three or four different options which spontaneously come to you. Circle the option you are intuitively drawn to.

5. Are any people involved? Who are they? Write down your intuitive response. (This point is not done for the challenges at the creation energy.)

6. Find out which emotions are locked here. Write down the feelings that come to you. If you have difficulty finding what the emotions are, write down a number of negative emotions in general and circle those you intuitively are drawn to.

7. Repeat if needed, as there may be many symptoms linked to the same cause or a symptom that has several different causes. Remember that healing takes different amounts of time for different challenges. Often the solution is a combination of the deriving, solving, and modifying your behavior, for example, to start exercising and deriving simultaneously. These various measures do not independently solve the symptoms. The combination of internal and external solutions is often what works.

No matter how much soul pain you feel, do not see it as something negative, but as a gift for you to know where to start looking to begin to heal yourself. Without the pain you would not know where you should look; you would not even know that you need to look. When the soul may say what it wants, including insights to you, often the external symptom releases. Through the pain you will stand up and become the best you can be. Not good enough for others, not good enough for your conditioning, but true to your soul at all times. The more true you are, the more soul pain you will heal out. You will then be more and more true in your relationship with God.

Flexibility

Why does everything seem impossible when it is not really so? We have probably all wondered over this issue at some point. There are in particular four reasons for this:

1. We are habitual people almost 100 percent and do almost everything as habits. This means that if you go from a mediocre state to a condition characterized by success, then you need to change what you do, think, and feel, how you react, and what you have conditioned in your soul. Only when this is done you can achieve the success you want. Very few have this insight, and most of us will therefore remain in a mediocre state.

2. No one has taught us how to create success in our life. You do not learn how to create success in school, where the time is mainly spent on learning theoretical things. If we could successfully introduce the subject of soul management at school, even the students who do not have parents that teach them successfully would be able to have part of this knowledge.

3. We confuse success with money. Although money often is a part of success, it certainly is not the only thing that is important. There are many individuals who have unlimited wealth but still no success. Money only enhances what you deep down believe about yourself.

4. We do not believe that what our conditioning sees as impossible is possible. We need to realize that we can really create what we want regardless of our conditioning and what others say. Flexibility is essential to create a balanced and rich life. Many believe that the more you control your life, the better life you get. But those who have the most balanced lives are those that can be flexible towards themselves and others. It does not mean you should do what others want and go against your inner truth, but rather you should do the things you should no matter how inconvenient it is. It means daring to go through your fears, which often say you should do things in a certain way to succeed. When you are locked in a habit, the creative power and the pure contact with God is not there in the same way.

Four points of flexibility that can help you along the Way

1. *Be flexible yourself.* Try to eat foods that you have not tried earlier. Try a new toothpaste, new kinds of clothes. Find everything you make a habit of and that is not really important in your life and break the pattern. The paradigm will want to keep you in the habit patterns, usually negative ones, and will do everything so you will not break your habit. The feelings that arise on these occasions are fear, apathy, frustration, and convenience. If you have any of these feelings when you try to break a

habit pattern, it is not your soul that is speaking, but your conditioning that is making itself heard.

EXERCISE 9.5. *Dare to break your conditioning*

Write up a clearly defined goal that you want to achieve, such as starting to eat fruit, if you have not done that yet. Write down the time and date when the change shall happen. When you then make the change, do not go back, regardless of what your paradigm gives you for negative signals. After one to three weeks, you will have broken the conditioning and you will be living a step closer to your truth, thanks to the flexibility you have created. Pick out one or two changes per day and do as above. Do not forget to always derive and solve the underlying cause to release the negative energy that is locked in your paradigm when you make your external change.

2. *Be flexible with others.* This does not mean that you do what others want you to do. It means daring to make contact with people whom your paradigm says you should avoid. Make contact with the individuals that you get the feeling are also looking for new challenges to grow as a person. The more flexible you are with yourself, the more you will attract others who are on the same track. If you then have the opportunity to work together with others also looking for new challenges, success is almost a fact.

EXERCISE 9.6: *Dare to face your fears*

Look up one or two new people a week that you want to have a contact with of any kind. Make sure that both you and they can get something out of your meeting. When feelings of inferiority or any other negative feeling arises in this exercise, derive and solve the underlying cause for the feelings to get the results you want.

3. *Be flexible with God and God will be flexible with you.* Many people are mistaken when they think that they must be perfect to be good enough for God. Then God reflects this image, and you only get answers for how to live up to being perfect for God. No man can win this match. Try to relax and trust that God is there for you when you ask for help. You will never have to be perfect in order to be good enough in God's eyes, and when you relax with this realization, God opens up even more to you. There are only two occasions when you need to examine yourself and God is partially assessed: 1) if you have deliberately hurt someone else; 2) if you without resistance allow someone you love to be injured by someone else. At these two occasions your power to God is closed until you make up and reconcile what you have done. This may be a deep and lengthy process, but it is possible to get through it.

4. *Be flexible and open to new insights.* The more you are open to new ways of looking at life, the more likely it is that you will get the insights you need. It is not that you have to do what others are saying to you, but the more open you are to new external information, the greater chance you have to succeed. What you then decide to do with the information is another matter, but you are now more flexible and open to change. Often we are so locked into old habit patterns that we do not even allow ourselves to look at these possibilities. Most contradictions between people about race, religion, and so forth are conditioned ways of looking

at each other, having nothing to do with our internal decision making but rather with the conditioned decisions going from generation to generation. Challenge yourself to start making decisions based on your insights and not on your conditioning. Our conditioning is unfortunately so incredibly controlling that we automatically often choose the political views and religion we have received through our environment without reflection.

Vital Insights

Life is a lot about insights. The difference between an insight and a paradigm is that the insight comes to you from God, through your intuition, while a paradigm is created by someone else to be used by you, but unfortunately often against your will. As long as we live through our insights, no harm can be done, for God never gives us insights that harm ourselves or others. The danger is when we confuse insights with conditioning and believe that our conditioning is an insight. As a remedy for this, I have created a program with thirteen insights that you can use to live your intuitive truth and not the conditioned reality which unfortunately is so wrong for so many. Below are the thirteen insights that you can take with you every day to help you grow into the person you really want to be. Read these insights one to two times a day to really begin to process the often negative conditioning that you want to get rid of.

1. I am good enough as I am. It is so easy to see this purely intellectually, but it is not until you see it as an inner soul truth that it will really have the effect you want it to have. By daily reading this, you will be confronted with all the thoughts and feelings inside of you that do not match this. You will have the opportunity to see all the negative patterns that have steered you in your life. Write down the negative patterns that rise to the surface, and take help from the Soulbalance method to solve the underlying cause for good. It is not until you are ready to invest in new ideas and create a new path that these old patterns make themselves heard. We have learned to ride a bike as a matter of routine, and it becomes part of our makeup, whether we like it or not. Similarly, our negative blockages are conditioned. We must dare to change direction to discover our limitations.

2. *No one else can decide whether I am good enough or not.* Many of us have become so heavily conditioned that we believe that we must be good enough for others to be good enough. Nothing could be further from the truth. You are of course good enough, regardless of what others think about you. If you do things to make your parents proud and to be good enough in your employer's eyes or in the eyes of a friend, you must do as they please to have a value. Realize now on a deeper level that this can never be a real truth; it is just something we learned from our parents and others around us that they, in turn, have learned from others. You are good enough to just be, no matter what anyone else is trying to convince you. See also the patterns you are confronted with here, saying that you are not good enough for others. Write down what they are and dissolve the underlying cause in the same manner as in insight number one.

3. *For God we are all equal.* Before God we are all equal, regardless of gender, race, religion, and sexual orientation. That so many of us do not believe this has nothing to do with God. God is the energy behind all creation, and we are all linked to this origin, which means we all are good enough for God. All allegations that some are more worthy than others are created by different human egos to give them a short-term satisfaction to dominate others. So if someone tries to push you down in any way, it has nothing to do with God.

4. *Regardless of religious affiliation, I am good enough before God.* This of course is valid if you are an atheist, which need not be a denial of God but rather a denial of religion as it is used today. You can be atheist but still have a faith, a divine faith, which links you more to God than to a religious leader. An atheist can be, like me, someone who is looking for something spiritual but does not know what he or she is looking for. Many people can be atheists because of their relationship to the traditional religions, but really have a strong spiritual faith. I have several clients who see themselves as atheists but believe in something greater, an energy, a force, the universe. They are what I call believing atheists. You are good enough, whatever the church says. It may sound easy in theory, but many of us are so full with religious repression, either in this life or from past lives, that I really must stress how important it is that we feel good enough for God deep down in our soul. I have had many clients who have been religiously oppressed in this life (yes, even in Sweden) or past lives. When we solve these blockages, usually numerous symptoms such as anxiety and inferiority disappear.

5. *I am neither better nor worse than anyone else.* If you think you are worse than anyone else, you need to strengthen your self-esteem, and if you think you are better than others, you need to review how your ego controls you. This does not mean you cannot create more success than others, for you can if you want, but your human value is not higher because of that.

6. *I have a choice every day to make the best of my life.* So many are stuck in a strong victim mentality where we think that others are responsible for how we feel. It can to some extent be true, but as long as we do not make the best of life, regardless of external circumstances, healing will never take place. You can choose which thoughts you would like to have today; you can, to some extent, choose how you feel; and you can now solve your internal soul blockages with the help of the Soulbalance method. There are no excuses for not taking charge of your life. Take a moment to see what excuses you have not to succeed in life. Solve the blockages using the Soulbalance method and decide to work yourself free from the victim mentality. It is only you who can change the image of whether you are a victim or not.

7. *My conditioning is my biggest enemy.* By realizing that your conditioning is only how you have been taught to see the world and yourself, you can get an understanding of why you react and act in a certain way. It is not really your true self, but your true self has become so suppressed that it no longer has a chance to express itself. When the pressure becomes sufficiently strong, you will not be able to live with your conditioning anymore. Many see this as a life crisis where they cannot continue in

what, for them, are old, deep-rooted habits. But really, there is no crisis; instead there is a very favorable condition where the soul finally gets a chance to have its say so that you can grow into the person you really want and can be. Sometimes the paradigm is so strong that you are completely stuck and do not see any light at all. Try then to realize that your desperation is really only the soul crying for help and appealing to you to change your life. What can be a bit tricky is that you need to make the changes and then feel good, not feel good first and then make the changes. The mistake many make is that they are waiting and waiting to feel good to get the right motivation to start their journey, but the healing will occur when you make the journey. It can therefore be completely pitch black until you make the change, and then it becomes light very quickly.

8. *My soul with my inner truth is my biggest supporter.* Your soul always wants the best for you, whatever your conditioning says or others say. Yet many chose to ignore what their souls are trying to say to them. Often we help everyone else before we really listen to what our soul wants. The paradigm has a tendency to always make us feel unwell, selfish, evil, etc., so we walk around with a guilty conscience about what we missed doing to be good enough. Your pure soul, free from the paradigms, never gives you criticism; the soul is constantly looking for solutions on how to help you grow and become whole. So stop listening to your paradigm, no matter how nasty it is. Your soul knows that you are good enough; now it just has to get this information to the whole of your being for the healing to happen. Imagine you are sitting in a meeting and you feel less worth than others. Is it true? According to your

paradigm, it is true. But your intuition knows that this is not really the case. Now, it is up to you to understand this, so you will feel more and more secure in yourself. When you encounter resistance, derive and solve it with the Soulbalance method.

9. *I do not have to try to be good enough for someone else.* This is perhaps obvious to most of us on an intellectual plane, but why do we not feel so deep inside? If we never have learned that we are unconditionally good enough, our conditioning seeks affirmation all the time. It is not until your soul has realized this that you can start to live a free life where you do what you want regardless of what others think. It requires a tremendous courage to live this way, but once you have made up your mind to really be true to yourself, there is no turning back. The soul has then made sure that you cannot take a step back into the old conditioning, but instead it is high time for you to be your true self, with a soul that wants to support you to realize your dreams.

10. *A crisis is a temporary condition.* Everyone goes through a crisis sooner or later. It is not something you want to experience, but it is a temporary state that sooner or later will disappear. If you are stuck in life and do not see anything positive, it is a temporary state that can be solved. Sometimes it seems to be permanent, but you can still get out of it. The problem with a crisis is that you can be at the beginning or end of it, and in both cases feel that there is no end to this misery. Since you do not know where in the process you are, you can be close to getting out of it, but because you do not see it, you think you are down and out for good. Just when you heal your locked soul crises, which must come to the

surface to heal, it can sometimes feel quite hopeless, although it really is a temporary healing crisis you go through.

11. *I dare to dream every day about what I really want to achieve.* Dare to think about what you want most. Dare to invest heavily in your dreams. View in front of you what your dream life looks like concerning finances, health, and relationships. When you have the ability to dream about something you really want, you also have the ability to achieve it.

12. *I act as if my dream is real.* Visualize yourself making decisions that bring you closer to the dream. Once you start to take action to realize your dream, it is just a matter of time before it is realized. So many companies, and other successful projects, have started with a dream of one or more people. Without that dream, their businesses or ideas had not been created. Many people say, "Others can do it, but not me." It is precisely such limiting thoughts that everyone has at some time but that successful people have ignored. Without ignoring those thoughts, the conditioning and opinions of others would have put an end to many of the world's large companies, relationships, and everything else that seemed impossible. If everyone had ignored their dream and lived their conditioning, we would have never left the Stone Age. So dare to invest in life and in your dreams.

13. *Life is a miracle, and I am a part of it.* One often says that the birth of a child is a miracle, with all the incredible change that happens between conception and birth. Everything is so amazingly arranged that only a higher power could be behind this. But what happens when the baby-

miracle grows up and becomes a teenager? Suddenly the child is a burden to society, and many believe that these children are not good enough. The belief in miracles has vanished and we try to find logical explanations for everything. But everything cannot be proven scientifically. A miracle takes place with people who use the Soulbalance method. It is God's gift to us when we use our intuitive ability to find how we can heal ourselves and others. When we get the insight we need from God, we are ready to heal ourselves. No area is really too large or complex. By being open and believing in miracles, you are also wide open to this kind of healing. Hope has solved much for so many. Never give up your dream of actually getting what you want out of life. It is your internal expectations and truths that create your life and gladly show what it can give you. We have much more influence in this process than we ever dared to hope for. We are all children of God and through God everything is possible, even what looks impossible.

Chapter 10

You are Unique

Remember that you are unique. You can create anything, no matter what you or anyone else thinks or says. There are many examples of people who have managed to create huge success from nothing. Two examples are Warren Buffet and Bill Gates, both of whom began empty handed. People get attracted to unique people. Throughout history we have either been attracted to or repelled by individuals who dared to show their unique gifts. Some have gifts that we want, while others have gifts that we absolutely do not want. What these individuals bring to life is our thoughts about our own unique selves. You may feel deep inside that if these people can succeed, so can you. The one that you distance yourself from makes you realize that you absolutely do not want to be like him or her.

We can all find our unique gift in order to attract what we really want. We are as unique as successful businessmen, sports or music stars; we just need the courage to live our inner truth. The problem for many people is that they do not get to express their unique self, but only work in an environment where they might be confirmed because they make money, but where they are not true to themselves. The challenge, therefore, is to always be your unique self. If you do not live in the flow with your unique self, you often live following someone else's standards, and no one really wants that deep inside. Do not be a copy of others. Instead, create something that leaves room for you to express your unique identity. Many people believe that they need to fly to the other side of the globe or get divorced to change. But do not have to go to India and meet a guru in order to find your unique self. You can create your own balance, instead of someone else telling you what to do and be. You can obviously make use of others' knowledge and insights, but sooner or later you will need to adapt them to your own unique soul ability to live the life you want. The mistake that many make is that they believe that if they copy someone's unique life, they are automatically unique also. But this is not the case. It is not until you are the best you can be, with your own unique abilities, that everything falls into place. You can also use your unique qualities to enhance your relationship with God, for your connection with God is unique. Many are trying to live by others' unique connection to God, but it works only temporarily, until you get the insight you need to see your unique relationship with God at all times. You can, of course, turn to the church, gurus, and coaches, but make sure that you have them teach you what you need to live your truth and not the truth they want you to live. What is unique about me is that I am very driven, I stick to my action plan I have put up, I dare, and I listen to my intuition. I listen to what others have to say, but then I do my own, internal assessment of whether I am going to use any of the advice or not. These are my unique qualities. To get what you want, it is high time you find your special unique abilities, not for me or someone else, but for you to grow as a person.

EXERCISE 10.1: *Find your unique self*

Write down five abilities that are unique for you.

1. If you find an ability, but you are not sure it is correct, just ask your intuition if it is right or not.

2. Circle the correct answer.

3. If the answer is no, proceed until you find your five unique abilities.

4. Carry them with you in your mind wherever you go and whatever you do.

What should you now do with your unique qualities? There is plenty to do. The abilities you get from God are unique to encourage both you and others in your development. Nearly 100 percent of all communication takes place on the soul and emotional level, and the interaction is between these. Say that you come to the conclusion that you have a very special ability to sing. When you use this full out, your feelings and your soul will be in unique harmony, and thus you get more power to achieve precisely what is right for you. God will strengthen this and give you what you want, no matter what your conditioning or others say. However, if you are trying to do things that are not in harmony with your intuitively found unique abilities, it can create a lot of negative vibrations in your entire energy system, which consists of your body, your thoughts, your emotions, and your soul. There are a lot of individuals who are trying to achieve many things whose abilities are not unique to them in association with God. I tried myself for years to perform in a certain way to make my parents and others around me happy and satisfied. Yes, maybe they were happy, but my soul hungered for so much more. Finally I understood what I should do. I would share with you the following insights: 1) that we all are unique no matter what our conditioning and other people say, think, and believe; 2) that all individuals can achieve the insight that they really can heal themselves and others if just the belief in God and the universe's positive forces are there. This is what I can and will work with the rest of this life. When I work with what is in conformity with God and my unique abilities, everything falls into place.

For me it meant a great relief to let the paradigm go that I must live up to my parents' expectations. It was not so much what they told me, but what they felt and thought about themselves that was conditioned into me. In their world everything should be secure and safe. A permanent job at a medium-sized company where you knew what would come the next day was what they felt most comfortable with. Everything I wanted with my life was not in resonance with their expectations. When you do something that goes counter to what the soul really wants, it creates chaos within you. In my case it created deep depressions and brought with it a host of other negative things. This is not what one should have to live with, either you or me. So think carefully. What is it that you really will do with your life? What are your unique qualities that will be useful both for yourself and for others? To search for what is unique absolutely does not mean that you need to imagine yourself being a CEO or anything else that others determine is successful. The important thing is that you do what is right for you. It makes no sense and is definitely not healthy to just live up to others' expectations. No one else can or should determine what is best for you. If someone tells you to do something but it does not feel right, you just say no thanks. This may mean that you stop saying yes to every family dinner, or that you do not accept everything your boss tells you to do. When you are changing, your environment is going to react, because others are accustomed to the behavior that your conditioning usually lives up to. If they say they do not like that you change, you should just ignore it and continue to evolve. Once your changes are complete, they will not have any criticism of you anymore, or you might have by then a different job or relationships. Because your behavior is new even for you, it can easily be struck down by your conditioning or condemnation of others' opinions. Rely on the response you get when you feel your unique qualities in exercise 10.1 and carry them with you wherever you go. The awareness of your unique abilities can make you understand that you need to do something you never have done before. Remember that your unique talent perhaps has lain dormant for a long time. It may need to be trained up some before the world understands what you have come up with. Once you have become accepted, you can exhibit the same behavior as before you became accepted, and then suddenly be perceived as unique, although it is not you who have changed anymore, but the outside world that has changed its perception of you. Take, for example, a program such as *Idol,* where unknown singers must fight for their unique abilities. When they are well accepted by others, the door is wide open, although they really had just as much to offer before their celebrity status. My parents often told me how great others were. But they never said I was great, which meant that I did not experience myself as any good. There is no excuse in the world for this behavior, for if your parents constantly repeat to everyone else that they are fantastic and not you, you perceive it as if you yourself are worthless. I tried to do something good, but never got any praise or appreciation. Perhaps sometimes when I have told them how worthless my childhood was, they have been able to squeeze out that I actually was good enough. But it has not felt real, as if it was an emergency solution for them to escape the confrontation without losing their dignity. Their actions made me prioritize myself last for many years because I myself carried a picture of how great everyone else was. I tried to be just as good, to be accepted in my parent's eyes, but it was really only a way to compare myself with others' unique abilities, which my parents for me so inexplicably admired. It was not until I realized my unique qualities and became free from the need to be good enough for my parents and others that I really began to live. Live *my* life, and no one else's. I had gained the insight that I must dare to be free and be myself regardless of what anyone else wants for me or thinks of me. Since I started to develop my intuition and really live my unique self, I have attracted many positive situations that involve me and others. I have also attracted a huge amount of criticism from some who do not want and cannot accept what I do. That does not mean I made a mistake, but rather it is a confirmation that I am making the right change; but, unfortunately, this scares some people who are negative about change. They then respond with criticism. In such situations I need constantly to let my inner critic heal. Then the external criticism does not have an effect on either me or anyone else that I should and can help.

Improve your Self-Esteem

To get out of the feeling that you cannot even dare trying to bring out the uniqueness you have, you need to improve your self-esteem. Your self-esteem is your unique tool that says you are good enough no matter what anyone else says or thinks. Self-esteem should be natural and a product of your parents' unconditional love for you. If you have not received that love, which almost nobody has 100 percent, your self-esteem has got a crack in it. As an adult, you can heal this poor self-esteem through to the realization that you do not need to be good enough for anyone except yourself. You are good enough for yourself and you are good enough for God, no matter what you or anyone else says. With good self-esteem, you are now ready to develop your unique qualities. For example, when you give a speech, you just need to be good enough for yourself and God, not for the audience. With this realization sunk in, you become relaxed in all situations. However, if you do not feel safe and calm despite the fact that you even know intellectually that you are good for yourself and God, then do exercise 10.2. It is designed to help you see how unique you are. In order to see how unique you are, you need good self-esteem. This can easily be seen as impossible if you have never had good self-esteem and therefore are not able to find your unique qualities, or if you feel you do not have something unique to show and thus confirm your poor self-esteem. This exercise is designed to break this particular pattern and give you access to a strong sense of self-esteem that can then permeate your entire life.

EXERCISE 10.2: *To break the negative paradigms for good*

1. Derive with the Soulbalance method where the uncertainty feeling comes from. Does it come from this life, past lives, or the creation energy? Circle the option you are intuitively drawn to.

2. If you have circled this life, feel intuitively and write down the age you get. For traumas from past lives and the creation energy, you do not need to find any age.

3. What happened? Write down what comes to you.

4. Are there any persons involved in the incident? If there are, write down the names that come to you. (This point does not involve the creation energy.)

5. What feelings are connected to the trauma? Write down your intuitive response.

6. Replace this feeling with a positive affirmation: "I am good enough in all situations regardless of what others think."

7. Repeat the affirmation ten times, three times a day, for three weeks, and you will be more confident when you face other people.

8. Repeat the exercise if necessary in an area that is a challenge for you at that time.

No one is worth more than you in your life, no matter what your conditioning says or what others say. This means that if you feel inferior to other people, it is from conditioning created by yourself and others, often while you were growing up. All human beings are born with equal self-worth. Then societal values and norms begin to indicate that some are better than others. But when you realize at all five levels—the physical, mental, the emotional, the soul, and the spiritual level—that you are just as worthy as others, you will get a calmer attitude towards challenges that makes you feel you can cope with anything. Remember that no one is worth more than you. If you have an imbalance at any of the five levels—for example, the soul level, and you do not think you are worth anything—you can show a strong facade on the mental and physical level but your imbalance will be felt nonetheless. When you have worked out your imbalances and blockages at all five levels, people will accept you whether you are successful or not, because what you send out vibrates outwards at all levels. The feeling of not being good enough is often linked to the authorities—authorities that usually symbolize the parents' steering of you. Even after that our parents have passed away, many struggle with the feeling that they are not good enough as they are. The memory of childhood has really nothing to do with whether your parents are still alive or not. You can still be damaged from your conditioning even when the one that gave it to you has left this earth. You may have to develop your faith that you are good as you are and explore your negative conditioning in this area, even if your parents no longer are alive. In some cases, blockages are linked to past lives and to authorities in past lives with a conditioning you often are completely unaware of. It may be that you had some kind of blockage with one or both of your parents from a past life. In my case, I know that I have had many challenges with both my mother and father ranging thousands of years back. In some cases, it is also so that we may have been our parent's parents with all the consequences that implies. If you feel an unnatural, heavy responsibility for your parents, this scenario may apply to you. But in this life, no child should need to take responsibility or the burden for their parents' lives and feelings. Derive the paradigm with the Soulbalance method for solving this issue.

Alienation

If that is how you feel on the outside, it is not you who is wrong. It may be that you have a unique link between the soul and the spiritual level that makes people feel you are a little different. When you try to be like everyone else, you lose the connection to God, and you will not feel less different, but probably only more off balance than before. The solution is to dare to see what is unique about you and dare to be yourself fully, even if it means you are not like anyone else. Eventually you will be secure in yourself, and then others will be attracted to you and what you stand for. People who feel different often have great challenges on just the soul and spiritual levels and often think about existential issues. The surroundings can be unsympathetic, and doctors or psychologists who are not interested in these dimensions may say that you must get your act together or take antidepressant medication. But this is not enough if you yearn for answers to existential questions. You will not achieve balance in life until you take hold of these issues. It may be the most important journey you go on, your existential journey during which you discover your unique purpose in life. Not everyone has challenges on this plane, and many can live a good life in a rather simple way. But many are struggling just with their existence, with what the meaning of life is. Then it is not sufficient just to get one's act together and think positively. But there is hope for all of us, and now I know that you can heal through the Soulbalance method. During the last three years I have developed the Soulbalance method so that some clients, in turn, could go on and help others to heal themselves. The more you use the method, the more you will be able to live according to your inner truth. You will develop your intuition and your healing techniques to such an extent that you no longer can or want to act to live up to others' standards and expectations. Progressively, you become more and more true to yourself, and what is unique to you will stand out clearly. Now you decide about your life.

New challenges

When you are on the way to really satisfying what your soul wants and realizing your unique self, continually search for new challenges – not pushing down feelings that are uncomfortable, not trying to be good enough or to satisfy someone else's needs. No, simply because you want to get the best out of life, despite your conditioning. The more you go from a completely conditioned life to a purely intuitive life, the more you discover and appreciate life's gifts. Such a small thing for many as seeing and hearing the birds chirp and play is a wonderful experience in itself. But as long as we are stuck in old, ingrained patterns that are defined by limiting conditioning, it is difficult to see such things. Of course, we can force ourselves to look at birds, we can force ourselves to try to appreciate life, but it is not the same thing. No, this is about the magic when you start to dare living instead of worrying about all the details. If we worry over everything, we are constantly on alert, and it is an expression that things are not as they should, which can lead to burnout and depression. When you start to heal yourself, there will be no room for these limitations. You are now a person starting to live in the flow and who refuses to let your negative self-image ruin your life.

Four ways to have Challenges in Life

To actually create the balance and freedom you want, it is good to begin to find out what works and what does not work in your life. To assist you further in the process, I have developed a way through which you can easily find out what you need to do to win at all levels in life. It is based on the following four points, each of which is for an area in which your main problems may lie. Each point's problems are solved with a little different approach.

1. *You are aware of problems/challenges at the physical level.*

You know you have challenges at the physical level. It can be anything from weighing too much to not having any money. You can see the problem, you know it is there. A great way to handle problems in this area is to create an action plan for what must happen if you want to lose weight, get a better paying job, and so on. It is also wise to derive the underlying cause through the Soulbalance method so you do not encounter problems once you change your habits. Often you can make a temporary change on the physical level and get good external results, but it is not until you actually solve the underlying cause of the physical problem that you can make a permanent change.

2. *You are aware of problems/challenges on the subconscious level.*

You know you have challenges that you cannot handle, and they are not physical but are more on a soul level. You may be struggling with poor self-esteem or are always afraid. You cannot physically see this, but you know it is there. Sometimes such fears can be linked to a physical symptom, but it is not necessarily so. You are in all cases aware of where you have your challenges. Here you can also solve the underlying cause through derivation with the Soulbalance method.

3. *You are unaware of problems/challenges at the physical level.*

You exhibit physical symptoms, but you do not know the reason. It can be everything from financial challenges to not realizing you are overweight. The solution here is to create awareness about yourself so that you can solve these challenges. Here, you must with the help of the Soulbalance method train your intuition and take it to a higher level where you start looking for things even if you do not know if you have challenges with them (but they are there). The more you train, the more secure you will be with your intuition. And the more secure you are with your intuition, the more guidance you get from God. Suddenly, when you least expect it, you will have developed your intuition to a level where you get advice from God on how to solve things that you did not know you had problems with. The reason that problems can be solved in this way is that all the information needed is in the universal soul, which is available for all of us to receive messages from if only we begin to rely on our contact with God.

4. *You are unaware of problems/challenges on the subconscious level.*
Here you are unaware that you have challenges in your subconscious. This is perhaps the most difficult place to find answers on what needs to be solved, because you do not even have anything physically to go on as you have in point 3, if you have found the right answer. When you begin to solve challenges here, you have taken your intuition to another level where you 100 percent start to trust your intuitive messages. Keep in mind that this is not a contest between individuals to show who is best, but to get to you what your soul needs right now.

The feelings you let free from your inner self when self-healing takes place can seem unmanageable. But remember that you may be releasing years or several lives full of pain in a very short time. There is no stronger, faster, or more liberating way to heal. You will never get more challenges to heal than you can handle at any given time. The closer you get to your inner truth, which is becoming clean of blockages, the more powerful things you get to deal with. It does not always mean that you will feel this detoxification more, but you will be more ready to handle the more powerful cleansing when you get it than you were, for example, a year earlier. What is so magic with the Soulbalance method is that it intuitively helps you find what you need to heal right now. Then God will do the rest, and as God is behind all creation, God knows exactly what needs to be done. So let go of all your control needs and just let the intuition empty what needs to be emptied. This can feel extremely uncomfortable and painful, but when healing is well under way, there is no way back to a life where the external control needs determine your happiness and the internal, negative, emotional blockages control you.

Dare to let go of your inner baggage so your control needs will let go of you.

Chapter 11

The way out of Stress, Depression and Phobias

No other human can heal you. You can get advice from others, but in the end it is you that control your life and your health. Your insights on how to heal yourself are the only path to balance. Overcontrol from, for example, parents and authorities discourage this process and cause even more problems, even if they intended to help. The solution is to let each individual take back his or her right and ability to heal. The responsibility goes from the authorities to the individual, and the individual transforms from a victim to his or her own life creator. It is not only the external control by others which limits you, but also your internal control needs. Many of us have some form of control needs, which means that we do not really live life to the fullest. These needs can range from having control of every bite we put in our mouths, to having the house cleaned in a very regimented manner. Two people can do exactly the same thing, but one does it because he or she is controlled by a control need, while the other has flow in his or her life and gets exactly what he or she wants out of life. The difference between being in the flow and controlling the flow is thin. Those who control their lives and break the flow do it for one reason: to try to conceal the feeling "I am not good enough as I am." The more you control, the less flow you get. The solution is to dare to challenge the need for control at all times by challenging the negative feeling which lies beneath the surface. The more you challenge your control needs, the more free you become, and you get more and more access to the unlimited love that we can all find within ourselves. To dare to let go of every little control requirement—such as not to double check that the doors are locked, or daring to let the children be involved in cooking even if you are afraid it could be chaotic—allows you success in all areas. When you really dare to let go, the soul is wide open to execute all your dreams.

If you have fear of death as a control need, it is only an external symptom for what is controlling you from the soul level. In what way does the fear block you? It blocks you so that you cannot reach the freedom to live life fully. So derive and solve the underlying soul cause. Once you have found the cause and begun to heal from the inside out, you can start living the exact opposite of your fear. In this case you will be able to engage in life fully and challenge your conditioning which claims otherwise. Dare to break all the control needs that try to keep your feelings locked. Once you begin to live in this manner, you will free yourself from all the internal restrictions that block you. This can be incredibly challenging, because the emotions are often released very strongly and are suffocating in their own right. You cannot take any shortcuts to get rid of the negative feelings. It is precisely in this healing process, which is easy to perceive as a living hell, that the insights you need for further healing appear. Without the healing of the pain, you would never get these insights. Try to see yourself and your healing from another person's angle when it feels hopeless. When you have that self-distance, you are in the healing process. When you have derived an underlying cause such as death anxiety, healing always occurs even when the feeling that the blockage causes comes to the surface during the healing process. With the awareness and soul insight you get through the intuitive healing method, nothing other than healing is possible. It is thanks to your intuitive contact with God that this is possible. God's gift to you is your intuitive ability.

Your gift to God is to use your intuitive ability in the best way possible. Self-healing is such an example. A soul in balance is free from the need for control and severe anxiety. The liberation is often not perceived immediately when healing, because the soul needs to get out the blockages that it carries on, which may take a while. Do not let others decide whether you are on the right track or not. Your soul will give you the answers you need for just you and your soul.

My fear comes from four previous lives where I had been punished for helping myself and others. Since I was punished with death in all these cases, my energy system believes that I should not and cannot act to follow my inner conviction, for then I will be punished. It is as if the ground is removed from under my feet just when I am going to succeed in something. I feel zeroed, halfway between hope and despair and between submission and a huge capacity. In my case the only solution is to live and be true to myself and God no matter how scared I am. When I dare to break the negative control behavior, I get huge power to do what I should and want to do on earth, despite the fear. But if I do not use my abilities, I destroy my life, never being truly true to myself. I have now realized that I have no choice. I will go for life no matter what my conditioning or others say to me. I am now ready to be the best I can. It feels scary, but at the same time enormously liberating, to have determined to never let myself be steered by fear again. This does mean that I am free from all fears, but I am prepared to do what I shall do and want to do, despite the fears. To keep our internal negative control needs in check costs three to four times as much energy as to unleash them. It is like a stopper in the drain which slows the flow of water. Therefore, your task is to challenge yourself and really find these negative blockages which you may be aware of, but unfortunately are often unconsciously present in your life. You know, for example, that you have a blockage when you are constantly tired no matter how much you sleep. You can try all sorts of other solutions, such as eating right, working out right, thinking right and believing you are right without it feeling true in your heart. Such an energy blockage often causes poor blood circulation without real physical cause. Many may have cold hands and feet, but it can also provide a host of other vague symptoms.

EXERCISE 11.1: *What lies behind your specific control needs?*

1. What is it you are so afraid of that is behind your control needs? It may, for example, be to really live life fully, to try to be the best you can, regardless of what your conditioning says and others say.

2. What is the worst that can happen if you drop your control needs? It can be, for example, to fail, not live up to your own and others' expectations. It can feel like this would be worse than dying.

3. Derive were the fear comes from using the Soulbalance method.

Stress, phobias, and anxiety

If you are a person who goes around being nervous all the time, it does not mean that there is something wrong with you. Your system stresses you until you do the adaptation of life necessary for the soul to get out its message. The farther you are from your truth, the more nervous you feel. Very many see nervousness as something negative, but it is rather a perfect tool to see what you really need to do to become true to yourself. Often you are nervous about just what you love to do. Say you are nervous to speak in front of large groups. Then it may be that you should learn and have a great talent for. People who are nervous just going outside the house often have a tremendous ability and talent hidden behind this blockage, and nervousness is just an outward sign of how important it is for them to do what they should. Their challenge will be to derive the underlying cause of the nervousness and free themselves from it so they can grow into the person they want and have the capacity to be.

Many people feel stressed. The most common advice concerning stress is that you should wind down and rest to achieve health. But the major cause of stress is all the blockages that are in the soul that we are not yet aware of. Without solving them, you can rest the rest of your life and still not get rid of these stress symptoms. The best you can do to manage stress is to derive the underlying soul cause of the trauma and release it. Then you can maintain a high tempo if you want and enjoy life without feeling stressed. If you do not solve your blockages, your inner stress is reflected in external stress. It is said that you should not make excessive demands on yourself. But if you create things that your soul wants you to create, you will not feel bad about the demands. The problem arises when you do something on the outer plane that you really do not want with your inner truth. In this collision, an enormous performance pressure occurs that can lead to stress-related diseases. This is because you are not living by your inner truth. So many people live their lives based on what they think others expect of them. Look at your life and try to see what expectations you have set for yourself. It may be that you have to be the best on your team or sell the best on the job. Examine the expectations and see if it is a question of being afraid of not being good enough. If your expectations, however, are about getting the best out of life according to your inner truth, you can reach them without getting burned out or feeling bad.

When you solve the blockages with the Soulbalance method, you can get detoxification symptoms, which are completely normal. After having found the blockage you can first feel low. That is because you start to process the soul traumas. But in the end you will really dare to fail, as you now know you are good enough whatever happens. For when you release your fears, the pressure from the inside diminishes and then also the pressure on the outside will disappear. With that, you can no longer do things that harm yourself and others. Then it is about choosing the direction. Many people talk about stress and burnout, but if you select the direction, you give your soul the key to self-healing. If you go against your inner truth on the emotional, mental, and physical levels, you get stagnation. But if you do what the soul wants deep down, even though you are afraid and have blockages, you will increase your flow of balance and success. When you are experiencing stagnation and feel that nothing works, go through each level. Test using the Soulbalance method to see the level at which your blockage sits. Is there a blockage, for example, on the mental level? It can be attended to and healed, so you can restore the natural flow again. The problem is that a small blockage on one of the levels can affect how the rest of you feel. Therefore, sometimes things that we with our intellectual perception see as banal can have an enormous negative impact on us. It is important to see the positive in the negative. To see the beautiful mountains, you will also experience the valleys. The "negative" is not there to break you down, but to help you gain insight and experience so that your soul can grow. When your soul then grows and becomes the best it can be, you will experience the positive. Then, the next "negative" experience happens and we just need to accept that it is a part of life. But do not go through the negative things with a fake smile; give yourself time to experience the strong feelings and heal your wounds. When a crisis occurs, we of course perceive it as negative. If you are aware of the crisis's different phases, it is easier to handle. The first phase is that you often feel calmness. After that comes the panic phase, followed by fear and grief. Finally, the ultimate healing occurs. If you are aware of the phases, it facilitates the self-healing. You cannot just skip the phases, for example, by pushing yourself in sports or taking pills. If you do this it avoids the message that your soul want to alert you about. If you press the emotions down in one way or another, you will not gain the insights you need. That does not mean, for example, that sports are wrong, but do not use them as a cure; make them a means to create the right physical conditions for balance. Realize that the soul always needs to heal its wounds. Crisis makes you grow, which is important to keep in mind when life is tough.

A phobia is an external symptom of an inner uncertainty that you constantly try to keep in check. The more you control, the more the phobic feeling locks itself in. When you experience a fear or phobia, it is just the tip of the iceberg that you encounter. The iceberg consists of a soul blockage, which can be fatal because it can have greater implications than the fear or phobia itself. Then you need to find the soul cause of the blockage and dare to change. By going through your fear and getting over your phobia, you can detect and resolve the soul block and achieve better balance in life. The same applies to other external negative symptoms, such as alcohol problems, anorexia, or gambling dependency. Even anxiety and other mental health problems are external symptoms sending error messages for you to find so you can begin to resolve things within yourself. It can be that you on the soul level do not think that you are good enough. When you then try to create what you want in your life, anxiety show up, not to hurt you, but to show that a major change is necessary. The anxiety can sit even deeper on the spiritual level, because you do not feel that you are good enough to exist for God, that you do not have an existential right to have it good. The solution in both cases is to identify the programming and let out the blockage which wants to come to the surface. You do that through deriving your problems with the Soulbalance method. Look at this life, past lives, or the creation energy, and feel intuitively where the blockage has its origin. When did it happen? What was it that happened? Were there any other persons involved? What negative feelings do you carry with you from the trauma? Once you have done this, you can focus on creating the life you want to have without blockages.

Allergies

If we have suppressed our true self through years of abuse by others and ourselves, we will sooner or later get physical symptoms showing that not everything is as it should be. An example might be allergies. So many of the allergies that we have are not true allergies, they are conditioned allergies. The symptoms are exactly the same, but the cause is not the same. Some allergies have a genetic background. You get them because of your genetic composition received by inheritance. The allergies are inherited from one generation to another. The conditioned allergies often do not turn up on an allergy test, but produce the same symptoms as a genetic allergy. To get rid of a conditioned allergy, derive the underlying soul cause through the Soulbalance method. There may be several reasons for the same allergy symptoms. Virtually all conditioned symptoms can be resolved. When a conditioned symptom is passed on to the next generation, it often becomes a genetic symptom apparent as a diagnosable allergy. Even for genetically inherited allergies, it is possible to deduce the soul cause, but the symptoms are often more inclined to become entrenched, which is not surprising when allergies go from a conditioned to a genetic inheritance. If a conditioned allergy is not addressed, it can then move on to become a genetic allergy. In my case, there were no allergies in the family, either on my mother's or on my father's side. I was also completely free of allergies when I was born. Because of my rough life and total self-loathing, I developed a variety of conditioned allergies, which meant I had symptoms as people with real allergies do, but the allergy did not appear in the allergy test. When I had children, the allergies switched from my conditioned allergies to the children's genetic allergies, which can be shown in a test. Once I learned how to derive and solve my allergies according to the Soulbalance method, my allergy symptoms disappeared rather quickly. What is important is to solve the underlying cause and then change the behavior that is conditioned by the belief that the allergy is real. In my case it was to eat, for instance, fruit, which I was allergic to, and at the same time derive and solve the underlying cause of the allergies. It is equally important to change the behavior as to solve the actual underlying cause. However, if you try to change the behavior without resolving the underlying cause, there is no improvement. The solution lies in the soul awareness you get to derive and solve traumas coupled with changing the negative conditioned behavior. The behavior perceives the allergy as the truth, though it really is not. When my allergies were solved, my children's allergies also disappeared. How is it possible? Because my allergies were caused by conditioning, I could solve them relatively easily, even if the paradigm put up enormous resistance so I would not change my life. Many parents and children are soul linked directly, which in my case meant that when I solved my allergies, even the children's were solved, thanks to our strong soul connection and because they had an underlying cause of trauma due to my conditioning. It was one thing that my allergies disappeared, but also to see that the children's allergies disappeared through my healing was astonishing.

What do you do if your parents do not resolve their conditioned allergies or other symptoms they have? It goes without saying that you can be free anyway, but a true allergy which is not solved by the person who has the underlying conditioned allergy is more challenging to solve. Derive and heal the underlying cause again and again, until it cannot affect you anymore. Do small behavioral changes when dealing with true allergies and expose yourself carefully to what you are allergic to. If the allergy is of a lethal nature, you should not expose yourself to what you are allergic to, but you can always derive and solve the underlying soul cause. We found out by chance that one of my children's so-called lethal allergies had resolved in this way, when the child by accident happened to get in contact with the allergenic substance, but the child showed no external symptoms at all. Trying this is not recommended, but for us it solved itself that way. We got what we needed and it turned out, as always before, that it was no coincidence anyway.

Important steps towards Healing

When it comes to your own expectations of yourself, it is important to look behind them and see whether they depend on other people's expectations. If so, they are not so positive. But that is, however, your inner soul's expectation—to be true to yourself to get the best out of life. If you are true to yourself, you can work hard without getting burned out or feeling bad. When you are aware of your pain, negativity, etc., and want to release those feelings, you have taken the first step toward inner healing. From this moment you do not, and your children (if you have them) do not, absorb the negative signals anymore. A positive soul decision has been made, and there is no possible return to the negative.

This is good for you individually, but the collective healing that occurs when more and more heal themselves is perhaps even more significant. With a world of individuals who make the right decisions for themselves, in harmony with God, the collective healing will be reality.

EXERCISE 11.2: *What feeling is to blame for your external symptoms?*

1. Find out what your external symptoms are that you feel you cannot solve. It can be anything from an allergy to control needs.

2. Immerse yourself and find the internal cause of your problems. You will know when you have found it, for it is the feeling that hurts the most, the feeling you have never dared to explore previously.

3. Let the negative feeling come to the surface and lose its inner controlling power over you. Make use of the Soulbalance method to do so. What is so amazing with the Soulbalance method is that once you have found the blocked feeling in your soul, the healing automatically occurs. My advice is just to accept it when it comes up to the surface, so you do not consciously try to hold back what you want to heal.

Unless you solve the feeling, you will not be free. Therefore, for example, financial advice or advice on how to lose weight does not work at all times. It is not unusual to see people who blindly follow training programs or dietary or financial advice without getting the results they want. A major reason for this is that each soul is so unique that general advice does not work because we all have subconscious blockages, which means that we cannot follow general advice. First when you have derived your blockages and dissolved them, the advice works. When, for example, advice on weight loss does not work, you put in extra hard effort to achieve what you strive for and become too controlling. It can result in a manic state that locks your energy. Dare to let go of the control and continue using your intuition. An excessive need for control is perhaps the biggest reason of imbalance and ill health. Have you noticed that it is often just individuals who are not balanced that attract these controlling situations? I followed, for example, a variety of dietary advice when I felt at my worst. I followed an ascetic diet without feeling better, while several persons around me lived without these restrictions and felt great. It did not feel fair, and I did not know why I did not get what I wanted out of the diet. It was not until I discovered that the clients I had that felt the worst had one thing in common: a social inheritance to control their lives. That this control need could have such devastating consequences was new to me. But when I taught myself and others to solve these control needs on the soul level, self-healing began to take place spontaneously. If you can access each individual's need for control by deriving and solving the underlying cause, you have come a long way. But it is not the whole solution. We must also challenge the controlling behavior on the physical level by going against the very familiar patterns many methods advocate in all spheres of life. Say that you, for example, go on a diet. Eat completely off the diet restrictions once in a while—not because the diet is wrong, but because you should not let the diet or anything else control you. The controlling behavior is usually there to protect you from discovering uncomfortable, subconscious, emotional blockages which are well hidden. When you begin to challenge these control needs, you will of course be confronted with these unpleasant feelings when they are about to leave you for good. But if you let them remain hidden and untreated, they will still cause tremendous damage. It makes no sense to ignore this, as the control needs will sooner or later manifest themselves in physical symptoms. My way to meet my need for control has been first to derive and make myself aware of the underlying soul cause, which almost 100 percent of the time comes from my mother's fears and internal constraints, which she conditioned me with. Certainly they were well meant, but unfortunately they were devastating for me. I have decided to break all the negative habit patterns that past conditioning has given me. An example would be to get up in the morning and not start with breakfast: I know it is best to have breakfast immediately, but I do the contrary to break the conditioning that I must do everything perfectly and in a controlled way to be good enough. Another pattern I can break is the perception that I must sleep at least seven hours to feel good. Sure, it is also true, but the energy loss it takes to make everything perfect so you can be good enough is far greater than what is caused by a little sleep deprivation. Eventually the control needs disappear and you are free to do what is best for yourself, without the controlling feeling. This is really great, and I am sure that most of our fears and control needs can be solved in this way. My devastating, almost lifelong anxiety was fueled by the need for control and disappeared when it was resolved. Control needs also lock your intuition, so the more you are free from your need for control, the stronger your intuition will be. Dare to break all your controlling behavior and be free. The more control needs you break, the freer you become, and the freer you are, the less need you will have for control.

How do you know what your controlling needs are? If you *must* do something to feel good or have balance, it is often a controlling behavior with an underlying negative cause. A life without the need for control is lighter, more abundant, with the feeling that you are living the life you want. A life free from control needs attracts balance and success. Being free of the need for control does not mean that you lose the power to do what you actually shall do. On the contrary, you are now much freer in terms of energy to create what you want. For the same reason, obsessive religious rituals do not work. They are based on the need for control. Instead, create your intuitive contact with God by letting go of these habitual patterns that do not lead to something positive. One of the main control needs is perfectionism in all its forms. Perfectionism is a way to control the fears that we do not want to come to the surface and bother us. The more you need to keep those emotions in check, the more perfectionist you will become. The feeling that is there inside you may be perceived as a threat if it comes out and heals, but it does even more damage in your subconscious, untouched, but not harmless—and oh so active. Are you a perfectionist? Must you do everything perfectly or require everyone else to do the same? Do you get stressed out by your own or others' mistakes? If you answer yes to one or more of these questions, you are suffering from the perfectionism syndrome. Make sure to be exposed to situations where not everything is perfect. Work through the feeling that comes up; release it. The key is to create momentum without having to be a perfectionist to be good enough. Being accurate is all right, because it is not anxiety driven and is often a necessity. Perfectionism, however, has really nothing to do with your success and is a sign of the need for internal and external destructive control to numb the pain of the experience of not being good enough. You can create success with accuracy and balance, but dare to let go of the perfectionist in you.

Four ways to a Happier Life

Everyone has a right to be happy, but if you have not got that right from your parents' inner happiness, you can create it by:

1. Overcoming a major crisis. For example, if you have overcome homelessness or a disease which is lethal, you can put yourself in that state. "I've survived this, now I am living my life to the fullest" may be an attitude that arises from such occasions.

2. Achieving something truly great. Not necessarily something big for others, but something that means much for you, for example, daring to stand on stage before thousands of people though you have suffered from social phobia (which, incidentally, can be solved with the Soulbalance method).

3. Being true to yourself. The more true you are to yourself, the greater sense of happiness you will achieve. This does not mean you walk around with a constant smile, but it means that you constantly live in a state where you create greater and greater possibilities for happiness.

4. Creating and ultimately feeling 100 percent love for yourself. Surely it can be easy, but I have not yet met anyone who has felt 100 percent love for himself or herself. But striving to get there makes you feel more and

more happiness, not because you are trying to be happy, but because you are simply accepting the feeling you are currently encountering. It is perfectly okay to feel happiness, but also to feel other feelings that we often perceive as negative. Derive and dissolve these feelings with the Soulbalance method and you will get closer and closer to the state all want to achieve, although we might not want to admit it to ourselves: unlimited love for ourselves.

Ego versus Wholeness

Healing is always something between you and God, no matter what anyone else says and thinks. No one else can affect how the healing should happen. The only thing a third party, such as a coach or therapist, can do is to make you aware of what it is you need to heal. When the person gave you that insight, your healing spontaneously happened when your soul received the recognition it needs. The more you can relax in the trust that God is behind this, the more easily you will heal. It is not that God is trying to be mean to those who have no confidence in the process, but the realization that trust is imperative to healing is important. With this understanding we will stop focusing on ourselves, what we call the ego, and go more and more over to do the right thing for the whole. We are then on stage to enrich others, we build businesses to help others, and so on. The big difference between living with the ego and living with the heart is that with the ego, you expect that you should get something like money, success, happiness, and more. When you are working from the heart, you look for the enrichment of others. On the surface it may look exactly the same, but the approach is quite different. Most of us start with the ego as a starting point, and there is no shame in this. The whole of society has taught us that we are better the more we have, do, and make. When we then realize that this attitude does not give us what we want, then we are ready to leave the ego behind us. For some it may take years; while for others it takes weeks. Some never let the ego go. Do you want to create as much opportunity for internal healing as possible? Then it is time to drop the ego. But how does this work?

1. By giving away all your assets and living only on what nature has to offer. Maybe not an option that works for the most of us in today's society, but an option if none of the other methods work.

2. By giving away 15 to 20 percent of your assets to the needy without blinking. As long as you find it difficult to let go of the money, the ego is not gone. For many, this is not an option because we have a responsibility to our families' survival. To give away without taking care of ourselves and our family is inversely ego, where one tries to smooth talk the ego to get the divine connection. This does not work.

3. By creating something that truly enriches others. It can be anything from a business idea to starting a charity.

4. By never going against your intuition and really doing what your intuition says no matter how inconvenient it is. The fact is that you may need to go out of your comfort zone to grow to be the person you are spiritually capable of being.

5. By not doing anything to get others' attention. You do not build a company to get the kick of showing how good you are or go on the stage to be hailed as a superstar. If you are a superstar or have unlimited money, it is quite all right, but the purpose is not there.

6. By not worrying about what you can lose. The more secure you are in this, the less you lose and the more confidence you create. This is perhaps the most challenging way to go, but it costs nothing and will heal you immediately, as soon as you start to drop the fear. The biggest fear for most is the fear of losing everything. It is felt by both rich and poor and is in the way of optimal contact with God. Once we get rid of the fear, we have already won, for the internal success is a fact the second you made up your mind. If you would like to work with this point, you can derive the underlying cause of the fear and heal yourself with the Soulbalance method. Of course, you can combine these different variants with each other one way or another. But it is usually best to choose one of the points. Never judge someone who chooses a different path than you—for example, a wealthy businessman or -woman who created a company that sells products that are good and enriches others while he or she earns a lot of money. He or she achieves the criteria for internal healing only through this, but can of course choose to combine it with any of the other items. Another example is a monk who lives under point one, so he has no assets left, and thus achieves inner healing. The mistake we often make is to condemn others for not doing things the way we think is right to be a good person. This irritation is created by the ego and is often based on our seeing the internal and external injustice in what others do, which is a kind of envy. Focus instead on your self-healing, and you will be one step closer to where you want to be.

Negative basic Feelings

I believe there are five emotions that underpin how people act when we think and work in destructive ways. Each one of those feelings is negative in itself, and combined the negative charge is even more destructive.

Five basic emotions govern a person negatively:

1. *Hatred.* So many of us live with an enormous hatred within us – a hatred against others because they have something that you and I have not. Hate is stronger than envy and does not allow you to create your own future because it freezes your energy. Let go of all focus on injustices you have suffered and see your opportunities in life instead. Do not expect anyone else to help you, but see that as a bonus if it happens. You have your life in your own hands, so make sure to become free from the enormous burden that the hatred is. There are four ways to do this: a) create what you really want to, irrespective of what others do; b) do not try to live up to others' standards and expectations, but be the person you are; c) make sure you derive and solve all the envy you carry around; d) consider that no one can do exactly what you can; you are unique and there is no point to imitate others.

2. *Self-loathing.* When you do not get the success you want, hatred is often transformed to self-loathing. Self-loathing eats you up inside and out and is possibly the most damaging feeling you can encounter. How have you created such an enormous amount of self-loathing? The worse you knowingly or unconsciously have processed the violation you have encountered, the greater the likelihood that you carry this feeling. Self-

loathing is one of the biggest causes of depression, for who would not feel bad when someone is attacking you twenty-four hours a day? In this case, it is none other than yourself who creates the violation over and over again. There is only one way to get rid of it: to recognize that self-contempt never is your soul speaking, but always your conditioning highlighting the inequalities that it considers that you have been subjected to. Your task now is to separate what is really true for you and what your conditioning says. The difference is that your soul always has enriching things to give you, while your conditioning gives you what you perceive that you need to survive. But if your conditioning builds your belief system based on false messages that you believe are meant for you, it may end up really bad. From here comes the self-loathing that has been created by others' negative acts against you in the form of abuse, humiliation, or something else that makes you not able to be your true self. You can take yourself out of this. It is not a true feeling to hate oneself, and if it can be created, it can also be replaced. For best results, derive and solve these messages with the Soulbalance method, and you will be free in the soul to be the one you want and should be.

3. *Grief.* Grief is so devastating because it gives us such a negative charisma. Some call the charisma an aura, and if the aura is full of sorrow, you will not end up where you want, but only in different conditions and situations in which grief can be felt again. If you do not resolve the underlying cause of the sorrow, it will only come back to you in a powerful way. We experience grief when we do not get out what we want out of life. Certainly there is other grief that we all sometimes experience when something tragic happens in our surroundings. But that

is not the grief I am talking about. I am talking about the grief that makes you not want to wake up in the morning, day after day, year after year. The soul has really given up and you only live a physical life. If you live a life in full conformity with what the soul likes, you have no further reason to feel this kind of grief. Those who say that they are never happy because they cannot do what they want are just martyrs until they decide to actually dare to experience life fully. Of course, there may be things that prevent this flow, but they can be solved by the derivation of the underlying soul cause.

4. *Denial.* So many of us are stuck in self-denial. As long as we have this feeling, no healing can take place. It is not until we accept our challenges that we take a first step towards self-healing. It may be becoming aware of how our parents have conditioned us and realizing that we may not have received what we had needed from them. It is not easy to break this paradigm, to directly and indirectly go against our parents' wishes and unconscious limitations, but it is time to really grow as an adult into what you want to be.

5. *Inability.* We have been unable to achieve much, according to our conditioning. But really, we can do most things. Do not listen when the conditioning that claims you are not able talks. The idea of our inability is often just an idea that our parents had for themselves and that they have passed on to us. If is not your true self; it is really an illusion, and the illusion does not exist. Do not make the mistake and believe that your conditioning is you, but release yourself from these notions. How do you do this? a) Determine where you want to be with your life. b)

What ideas do you have conditioned about your inability that prevent you from getting there? c) What should you now do to free yourself from this negative conditioning? To see yourself in third person, from outside in, and really see what this conditioning is doing to destroy you is a good start.

EXERCISE 11.3: *What emotions control you?*
See which of these precisely named points affect you.

1. What makes them so destructive to you?

2. How will you solve this so that you become free of their negative impact on you?

3. Use the Soulbalance method freely and seek answers.

Decide right now to get rid of the negative and move forward. You can, and you can do it now. See how you grow as an individual with more and more insights when you heal yourself with the Soulbalance method.

Meaning versus Meaninglessness

Unfortunately many of us are struggling to have a meaningful existence. Life should actually be quite simple, but for many it is very complicated. It should not have to be so. It is not God's gift to you. Having meaning in life is essential. When life feels meaningless, there is no magic in the air, birds do not chirp, and depression is close. There are three things you can do to get rid of that feeling and really get to experience life as sweet as it can and should be. Of course, we all have good and bad days, but life should still be a celebration of humanity and what it stands for.

The three things you can do are:
1. Really take God's offer seriously. The divine power offers all the possibilities that exist if you only are open to take the chance. One would think that everyone would choose to invest 100 percent in life with the knowledge of this, but instead of going places, we often live in a mediocre state. Why is this so? We are so afraid to live to our full potential, so most of us turn off and avoid facing this option if or when it is offered. Would it not be better to just invest in life when you get the opportunity of a lifetime?

Unfortunately, we have learned after thousands of years that we should be subjugated to fit in, be good enough for others, not destroy what our families have built up, and so on. But if you never give yourself a chance to take advantage of life, God will not be able to help you. God only reflects what you deep down want and think about yourself, and if there is nothing positive to reflect, life will be negative thereafter. This does not mean that you need to be a superstar to really make things happen. What is needed is a decision that you cannot withdraw from life, a decision that you will never give up your dream as long as you live. In this environment, meaninglessness dies faster than you can blink.

2. Don't let yourself be discouraged by others' comments and opinions when you are going where you want. When others are living a meaningless existence, they often want to drag you down to the same

level as them, where day after day is devoted to meaninglessness. Make sure you have people around you who also strive to be the best they can. In that spirit, the meaninglessness will lose, for it attracts all those not trying.

3. Find your great love for your work. We know what happens if we are together with someone we do not like in a relationship; it never works in the long run. For some reason, we believe that we can have a job that we hate and still keep the relationship alive. It will not work. So find your love in what you work with, and you will feel completely different than if you just got a job to survive. Of course, sometimes we may have to take a job to survive, but the dream keeps meaninglessness away.

If you or those you love struggle with meaninglessness, it could be that you or they do not give life the chance it deserves. The problem is that you cannot feel meaning and then create what you want to have; instead, you have to create what you want first and then the meaning comes. It is one of the biggest mistakes many of us make: we expect we should be positive and feel the meaning in order to create what we want, when the opposite applies. So really, you have no choice; go ahead and create what you want, whatever you feel right now. Maybe you are burned out or deeply depressed, states that many say are almost impossible to get out of. So many health-care resources are spent on helping people to suppress symptoms they did not want. But it is like trying to extinguish a fire only by putting out the flames coming out of the house or out of the woods. You must address the underlying cause of the negative state to get a lasting change. This cannot happen if you do something in life that you feel is meaningless. Both burnout and depression are external signs of internal meaninglessness that people with both of these two symptoms feel. When there is no meaning, your body and soul will sooner or later give you symptoms you do not want, so that you will make a change. Once you create meaning for yourself, the external symptoms are no longer required and health becomes a reality. Life has no meaning until you create it. By learning how to create meaning in life, our health care system would save a lot of money. No pill in the world can help you create meaning, regardless of what we want to believe. The meaning of life can only be created by a person who is willing to heal himself or herself. Do not see it as someone else's fault if you feel that your life has no meaning, no matter what you have been through. No one else's will to make you feel good will do the job. When you are ready to grab life and create healing, God can reflect this and help you get the results you want.

Imbalance and vitamins

I struggled for years to achieve balance in body and soul. A major challenge that I had was the imbalances that I had with vitamins and minerals. I have had, since way back, large imbalances in my mineral absorption, and it was revealed that I had shortages in some areas and a surplus in others. After years of vitamin and mineral supplements, no significant change had occurred recreating the natural balance in me. This means that I probably could have been eating right the rest of my life, or taken just the right supplements, without something positive happening with my health. Sure, you could, in a sample, then demonstrate that I had more balance in the short term, but I felt just as bad as before. I began to explore the area with the Soulbalance method and discovered that you can almost eat yourself to death on the right diet. Unless the inner soul is in balance in relation to one's vitamin and mineral absorption, you can still get and create imbalances. In my case it was the trauma caused by the existential threat posed by the English teacher who created the imbalances. The stress that this event triggered affected me internally and created a permanent stress blockage that ate up the vitamins and minerals. Over time the imbalance became just bigger and bigger, until it was shown in external physical form at the age of fourteen. No vitamins or minerals in the world can remove the soul trauma. You can process a trauma from two directions with the help of the Soulbalance method. One is to look backward from the trauma to resolve the underlying cause and become free from the negative emotional charge that is locked up. Another way is to start from your vitamin and mineral balance and see if it is good or bad. We are not talking about the physical balance but about the soul balance, the foundation of your ability to absorb healing energy.

EXERCISE 11.4: *Balancing your vitamin and mineral absorption ability*

1. Write down all the vitamins and minerals on a piece of paper and identify those you are drawn to, focusing on a surplus.

2. Do the same thing but focus on deficits. You have now found the imbalances you have in your soul that affect you twenty-four hours a day.

3. Now you can take your imbalances, and derive and solve the underlying cause.

I had an imbalance in my copper levels and derived the underlying cause by the Soulbalance method to the age of five, when I became exposed to the teacher's threats. The feeling that was locked in me was self-loathing, because who likes themselves if they are not good enough for God, although I at that time did not believe in God. Once the soul blockage was identified, my inner self could heal and restore the copper balance. I went through all the other imbalances and discovered that most were related to the trauma at the age of five, but not all. Some I had traced back to other ages or lives. The more we peel our "soul onion," the more balance we create. Sometimes we discover traumas and imbalances that we did not have the opportunity or awareness to solve a year ago. Everything has its time, and the soul helps you solve what you need right now.

The importance of Sleep

Sleep is really important to feel good, but so many are struggling with it. To get the best sleep possible you need to ensure that you are your own best friend and that you take care of yourself for better and worse. If you fight with a lot of "musts," where you must be good enough for others, you will not get the quality of sleep you need. "Must" has, unfortunately, an ability to make us dwell on a soul plane at night, and our sleep is not good until we have released our musts and done what we want. For some it may be sufficient with three to four hours of sleep to get quality sleep, while others need nine to ten hours to feel rested. To find your ideal number of hours of sleep, you can do a little test where you intuitively feel what is right for you—not what the doctors, neighbors, or others say is right for you, but what you feel is right for you right now. Over time, this can of course change, but it is sufficient to test yourself three to four times a year for this.

EXERCISE 11.5: *Find your true need for sleep*

1. Write the word "sleep" on a piece of paper.

2. Write down the number of hours you have slept, on average, per day the last week.

3. Now find out if it is too much or too little for you, or just right. Write down the three options on a piece of paper, "too much," "too little," and "just right," and identify what you intuitively are attracted to. Please be aware that this has nothing to do with what you intellectually think; it is your intuition that knows the best answer.

4. If you get too little or too much sleep: just write up three or four options with the hours to sleep, longer or shorter, and identify the option that you are intuitively drawn to. You have now found the number of hours of sleep that is best for you right now.

What many are struggling with is compulsive behavior which is concerned that you get too little sleep and that fear keeps you awake. It is especially common if you have a deadline to meet in the morning. The whole day becomes ruined, or you *think* it will be destroyed, by lack of sleep. The human being is created so that we can get through periods of sleep deprivation without it being harmful. It is rather the concern about what the lack of sleep can cause that ruins it for many. Here it is important to dare to release all control needs. It is almost always perfectionists who suffer from this condition because they believe that they need an exact number of hours of sleep or the right pillow to sleep well. Once you have this need for control, it is a sign that you press down the feelings that you do not want or cannot handle. If you have to be perfect to be good enough, you will always struggle with sleep, for no one can ever achieve the perfect day or the perfect life. Derive from where this feeling comes from in your present life or, in some cases, in previous lives. Once you find the time and the cause, you will sleep better because the neurotic sleep behavior is just a symptom of your internal concern. It may be that you have several causes for this challenge and then locate and derive them with the Soulbalance method until they are resolved. You have solved something much bigger than your sleeping problem, as you have healed a variety of blockages in your subconscious. If you are a parent with small children, you have surely on and off struggled with sleep deprivation when the child is sleeping poorly. Take a look at yourself rather than focusing on the child. What is it inside you that makes you and your baby not sleep properly? Derive the answer with the Soulbalance method and you will be surprised how much our own balance affects the child's welfare. This is not to put pressure on you, but it is an excellent opportunity to find blockages in yourself that you would not otherwise have found.

Chapter 12

Live your Dream

Free life or obligations? Basically, we should be free to create what we want regardless of what others think. In our lives, there is so much to be fixed, paid, and kept up with that the creative power does not get so much room. If you dare to explore what you want in life, you can find the way there—to a life where you feel free of obligations. You are the one choosing your future, no one else. Many want help in the process, but it is your thoughts, feelings, and soul connection that determine how it goes. If you choose to go into self-pity, you will, guaranteed, have a life of continuing failure. To get the contact with God that you really want, do things from the heart and avoid acting on the guilt feeling. With the heart you talk with God, while the guilt is talking with the ego. Many believe that the ego only has to do with grabbing money, power, and so on, although in many cases the ego more likely does things to relieve your guilty conscience. As long as you do things you feel you must do, you get out of touch with God—not because you are a bad person, but because you violated yourself and did not follow your heart. Therefore, two people can perform exactly the same action but do it for two quite different reasons, and the flow for these two persons will be completely different.

Think about when you did something good for someone else, but it felt wrong for you. You can do a lot of good deeds for the wrong reasons and really make a mess out of it. What can you now do about this?

1. See what "musts" you have in life.

2. See which of these you can convert to something you want. For example, you must go to work and feel offended by this idea. However, if you convert it to something you wish for—for example, that you really want to take care of your family with food and a roof over their heads—it is so much easier to do certain things that you first did not want to do. You have transformed something from a "must," which violates you, into something you want, and as a bonus you will be more and more true to yourself.

In the end you no longer feel you "must" pay bills, pay for social obligations, or give money to your children. The musts get turned into something you actually want. Your existence then becomes much easier, and the divine flow increases with your self-respect. Actually, there are no musts. To wash, pick up the kids at kindergarten, and cook are really not musts. You do it so that you can wear clean clothes and so the children feel good. You can convert all musts to something you want so you can live in balance with yourself and others. Is there something you do not want in your life? It is time to identify and get rid of it. And remember that a must for someone else does not need to be a must for you.

Below is an exercise that will help you be free from others' energy, right into your soul. When I coach individuals, we often see that they are not entirely free from other people's energies, but they carry forward a lot of other people's guilt and burdens. In my case, I carried the enormous guilt burden which had to do with my mother. All my life I had been taking in her heavy energies to save her so she could feel good. The only problem was that I felt so incredibly bad because of this that I often did not know if I wanted to live any longer. Buried under this weight lay my true joy, but it was only through the Soulbalance method that I could get to the bottom of the problem.

Many people carry others' burdens and guilt and will not or dare not do anything about it. This must be highlighted to help individuals heal. I tried myself to avoid the subject for years not to make my mother sad, but when I had children and they began to absorb my mother's melancholy attitude toward life, it was enough. They also got this melancholy from me, because I had inherited this approach to life. It was simply time to be true to myself, my wife, and my children, and not put my parents on a pedestal as I had previously done. Since I broke the contact with my mother, the whole family feels better at all levels, both physically and in our souls. I feel for the first time that I live my life, and not what my parents want or expect from me. When my father passed away a few years ago, I obviously felt some sadness, but the feeling of being free from all of his unspoken demands was much larger. Since I broke with my mother and my father passed away, my life is so much better. I never made these decisions in order to desecrate my parents, but because I had to do it to survive and to protect my family. If you are not experiencing this type of problem with your parents, I just congratulate you. But you can have other persons around you who drain you of energy and "infect" you with their negative attitude. The exercise below will help you get rid of whoever or whatever costs you so much energy.

EXERCISE 12.1: *To be free from who or what controls your life*

1. Draw six annual rings as on a tree, from the inside and out. Try to do the innermost ring around one inch in diameter and increase the diameter of each ring that will be added by one inch.

2. Furthest in, write down what affects you most in life. This may be a fear, a phobia, but also a neighbor, an ex, or yourself. In my case it was my mother. I wanted so badly to please her, so she ended up there. Trust your intuition when you do this exercise and do not let your conditioned thoughts steer your choices. Let go of all musts and write down what comes to you intuitively even if it is taboo for you or your surroundings. Now you need to be free, and honesty to your soul is needed.

3. Continue to write from the inside out. In my case, my late father was next, and then my phobias, fears, my poor financial situation, and my poor self-esteem. I myself was not even on the annual rings, but appeared first in eighty-ninth place.

4. Draw now a new set of rings and write how you feel that they would need to look for you to get balance in life. Normally you should have yourself furthest in, then possibly children, partner, and job. After that, perhaps, parents and friends.

5. Ask yourself what you need to change to get to the right image of point 4.

6. For example, does your mother-in-law steer your life furthest in? Stop going over for Sunday dinner just because she wants it, and dare to say no! If you then intuitively feel that this is enough, then you are done; otherwise you will have to take more action.

7. Ask yes-or-no questions intuitive to yourself and move forward.

Your internal Financial Conditioning

I meet lots of different people in my job. Most have one thing in common: poor finances or concerns about their finances. Most people in Sweden say they do not think money is important, but still money is steering their world 100 percent. My parents had stable finances when I was growing up. My father was, for a while, CEO for a large company, and my mother was not bankrupt, either. We lived in one of Sweden's most desirable areas, but still my parents taught me to think, feel, and live as if we were poor. In the end, this conditioning was engraved so deeply in the soul that I got a stomachache for the smallest taxi ride, or because the tomatoes were more expensive in my store compared to the cheaper price I saw in the paper. It may seem trivial to address this topic, but this attitude towards money ruled my life so that I could not create good finances for myself. Sure, my parents wanted me to be successful and have a secure income, but it was impossible when they had taught me that life is difficult. "What if things go wrong and you lose everything?" was thinking which had been a part of my life since childhood. This was nothing I wanted to pass on to my children, but unfortunately they came in contact with these thought patterns before I healed the negative emotional conditioning that I had carried around for nearly forty years. This conditioning can be inherited from generation to generation, and it is not until you heal it out that you are free. I have done it with the Soulbalance method, and several of my clients have done it as well.

EXERCISE 12.2: *To break negative financial conditioning in yourself*
We are financially conditioned deep in our souls. There are three variations on this conditioning: One is that you always have larger revenue than expenses. The second is that these two are equal. The third is that income is less than expenditure. You will always realize the conditioning that you carry deep inside the soul. It is not always what you want, but it is the financial conditioning that you carry deep inside the soul. In my case, I was conditioned always to have less income than expenditure. What is your situation like? You need to find out which of these conditionings you have. The exercise gives you the opportunity to become free from any adverse financial conditioning you inherited.

1. Write down the three types of conditioning:
a) revenue exceeds expenses; b) income equal to expenses; c) income is less than your expenses.

2. What conditioning do you have? Circle the one you are drawn to. Then you intuitively have found where your blockage is in the subconscious.

3. If you are not satisfied with the financial conditioning you found, derive it with the Soulbalance method to determine the underlying cause of it. As mentioned earlier, you need to find where each block is located,

what caused it, and which feelings are associated with this situation. Sometimes it is not even a situation but more a daily negative approach, as with my parents' approach to money.

4. Thanks to you going through this exercise, your negative conditioning will be solved in terms of energy and you can start to create the balance you want, where your income is higher than spending.

5. Now you have resolved this major challenge in terms of energy, but it does not mean that success will automatically show. You need to ask yourself the question: What do I need to do so that revenue is larger than my spending? Your conditioning will make itself known until you make both the internal and external changes required.

6. Write down three or four answers that you intuitively feel would be the right activity for your new positive attitude to money.

7. Identify what you really intuitively feel is right for you. If none of the actions is working, replace them with others and test them. Continue this process until you have found what you really should do.

Now you have both solved the blockage and derived how you should act for success. See now that you can create what you want by using goals and an action plan. In my case, it was to write this book and help as many people as possible to become free with the Soulbalance method. Here are three pieces of advice that you can carry with you on the road to success:

1. Decide what you want to create success with. Do what you really want with your life.

2. Do not let anyone stop you from achieving what you want. So many want you to stay in old negative habitual patterns that are convenient for them if you do not change.

3. Customize your solution until it suits you and the market perfectly. Dare to change what you do, and dare to face new challenges all the time.

Dare to go for your Dream

When you are free from your negative conditioning regarding finances, it is time to take a look again at how you can create your dream scenario. We have looked at your inner truth earlier in the book, but nothing is static, which means that you now are ready for a more complete picture of your life than you were in the previous chapter. The book gives you the tools that enable you to create sustained development and improved balance. I learned, and maybe you have learned, that if you only complete things, everything will be all right, but that is not anything to strive after. Sure, you can be ready with some subprojects, but life continues also the day after an exam or an Olympic gold medal. When I realized that we never really become finished, the performance anxiety I carried disappeared. I thought that I had to finish everything *now* to be good enough. The exercise 12.3 gives you a chance to see what your dreams may mean for you, and also what happens when you do not live the life you want.

It is so easy to choose right, but still so few choose the path that suits them. Do this exercise at your leisure and feel the two scenarios. Select then what is really right for you.

EXERCISE 12.3: *Choose and live your dream*

1. Imagine you are living in a fairytale world and can choose exactly what you want to do with your life.

2. View in front of you all you discover and develop about yourself.

3. Write down in detail what the picture looks like, how you live, what job you have, and what you do in your personal life.

4. Try to let go so you can really relax and live your way into the image.

5. Then create a picture where you are struggling and have it tough, where you live to be good enough for society, where you have lost all your dreams and hope.

6. What image do you choose? Of course, most respond that they want to live their dream image, but the fact is that few actually live the life they want. Are you one of them? With a little development and understanding of how we are constituted as human beings, we all can strive for and come much closer to our dream image.

There is a lot you can do to really create the life you want to have. We certainly agree that it is necessary that you act. Not to do anything is not an option. But you must also act in the direction that is just right for you. Here are three pieces of advice for success:

1. Choose what you want to do, not what others want for you.
2. Dare to go for your dream.
3. Remember that all dreams are coated with resistance. You only have to get through the resistance to get to the other side.

Dare to fail to Succeed

Have you thought about how much some achieve in their lives, while others just go and drag their feet behind them? In order to create strength and success, you need to grab what you want to achieve. Behind every idea and success is always a lot of effort, which we do not see when the success is a fact. What is your idea or dream you want to achieve? Have you decided to give it a chance? Behind every success is often also a variety of failures. Is it not time to dare both success and failure? When you are ready to fail, you are ready to create the success you deserve. I have found that it is through our failures that we grow most. It is perhaps not what you want to hear, but when you go for what you want, you will fail on the road to success. Your approach to what we call failure will determine where you end up with your life. If you are fretting with yourself for each failure, then that is what you carry with you, and that will create your life under the law of attraction. If you, however, have an open attitude to what we call failure, you will attract the positive into your life. This change is not something you can force, but it is an inner strength you will develop the more you take part in the Soulbalance method's ability to heal. Here are three pieces of advice for those who are willing to fail to succeed:

1. Go ahead and realize your dream today. Delaying it until the future is usually the same as giving up.

2. Do not let anyone stop your dream (yourself or others). It is so easy to find a thousand excuses for not doing what you need to achieve your dream. Do what you will regardless of your conditioning and others' opinions.

3. Make sure you create an action plan that you cannot back out on when you start becoming afraid to fail. The whole point of a plan is that you commit yourself to do something no matter what your conditioning says or what others' opinion are, according to point 2. Through the years I have worked with and helped thousands of individuals to a better life. It is always those who have a clear plan who create the best results for themselves and for others.

So now really decide to do what you will do. Not to decide itself is perhaps the biggest stumbling block of all. It prevents millions of people around the world from really exploiting their full potential. Are you one of many who constantly put things off to the future and think everything will resolve itself that way? Of course it does not work. The reason we postpone things to the future is that we do not want make a decision about something, and when we do not make a decision, it is impossible to create success. It is our conditioning that governs our lives. For the unsuccessful, there is often a great conditioning of indecision. Successful people make quick decisions and change their minds slowly, while unsuccessful people make slow decisions and change their minds rapidly. Which group do you belong to? Successful people also make mistakes, but they make as many decisions in a day as most people make in a year. Here are three points that you can take with you on the way to becoming a powerful decision maker.

1. What decisions are you facing that you want or need to make?

2. Will you make a decision quickly or slowly?

3. Be comfortable with the decision you make.

Creating success by letting the Ego go

There are two ways to create success. One is to rush its development. This happens when you let the ego control you and feel that you *must* create this success to constantly prove that you are good enough. When you really believe that you are good enough, you create a flow that creates attraction. You attract the people you need to realize your dream. There is a distinction between goals that are set by the ego and the goal set by your inner truth. Goals set by or for the inner truth so that you really can be one with the universe focus on enriching yourself and others. They have self-healing purposes and allow you to be more complete as a person. This point is incredibly important, and really underestimated. I previously had a need to be affirmed to feel that I was good enough. Since I had low self-esteem I searched for the affirmation from everyone all the time. I wanted to create success to show the world that I was good enough. The problem with this approach is twofold. One problem is that you always have to show that you are good enough and can never relax. The second is that whatever you create, the ego will never find that you are good enough. You will never be satisfied with life. The billionaire or a spiritual leader who built his business with the ego may never get what he really wants, namely, internal balance and a sense of getting God's unconditional love. Certainly God gives unconditional love all the time, but you must be able to receive it and accept it in order to use all its healing and intuitive power. When you release the ego, you come closer to God through that action. No matter where you are in life—a billionaire or a bum—you can achieve the same feeling being one with God.

To zero Oneself

To zero yourself is to believe in yourself in one instant, but not in the next. There will be two steps forward and two steps back = zero progress. Many people carry on this conditioning. I myself was conditioned that I needed to create success to be good enough, even though I felt I had nothing to offer. I was not good enough. You cannot create success with such conditioning, and it has been proven to me over and over again. It was like an invisible wall that hindered me all the time. Find out if you are zeroed. Ask yourself: Yes or no? Use your intuition for this. If the answer is yes, you can solve your challenges with the Soulbalance method. What is it that prevents you from believing in yourself? When you have found the basic cause, you can get rid of the negative force that holds you back. There may be more than one thing that is zeroing you, so just keep on looking until you feel you are getting the flow you want.

Genuine Gratitude is a way to get closer to God

Without gratitude for what you have in life, it is irrelevant whether you have much or little money, or if you are successful or not. There are so many people, sports stars and celebrities, who have everything, but without gratitude their life is not really happy. A good way to get used to showing gratitude to yourself and others is to take some time at dinner and say what you are thankful for. The more you express your gratitude, the more you get back with joy and success. It seems perhaps strange at first, but after a while the gratitude is a part of you at all times. I struggled myself with this point for a long time, for I felt no gratitude in my life. How could I feel gratitude when my paradigm said that life was a living hell? I tried to improve and show my gratitude with other methods of personal development, but because the feeling was not genuine, I did not get the life I wanted. You cannot create something in a fake way, especially not gratitude. Gratitude comes from within when you heal yourself from your negative conditioning. When the soul is healed, then gratitude will come; the gratitude that you have been able to heal yourself knows no borders. Life will still have its challenges, but knowing that you always carry with you a healing and intuitive power—God—cannot ultimately give you anything other than a genuine internal gratitude.

Time for Change

Most people I meet in the context of coaching usually want a change. But why is it that only a few manage to achieve it? For me to accept a client, I need to be convinced that the desire to evolve and go through all the fears is stronger in the individual than the pattern that keeps him or her remaining in an unwanted situation. These fears can be phobias or any other strong visible fear, but many times this is a conditioning that is more subtle and harder to detect. That it is difficult to detect unfortunately does not mean that the harm is smaller. In my case, I had huge obstacles to overcome, including panic about meeting other people, which as a teenager was reflected in the fact that I got drunk to dare to meet friends or to be intimate with the opposite sex. When I discovered the Soulbalance method, I new that I had no choice but to face my conditioning in order to succeed in becoming whole, no matter how scared I was and no matter how much pain would have to be freed to heal me. I have previously mentioned in the book that when you heal the pain, the same pain that has conditioned us must come to the surface and be relived. There is no other solution. If you have not been through this type of pain but are still stuck in life, you need in a similar way discover what is stopping you in your process of change.

The most common excuse for not taking charge of things is not having time. All people have the same number of hours in a day. But there is a huge difference between individuals, what they do during a day. Many never take charge of things head on, on the pretext that they do not have the time. Do you think it is the busiest people who complain that they do not have the time? No, it is all those who want to achieve balance and success, but who are so afraid to take charge of it that they blame the lack of time to avoid facing the challenge. I have coached a number of individuals who believe they suffer from time deficiency, but when you ask them to do a weekly schedule, there is always enough space to do new, different things, which can take them closer to their goals. We are all more or less products of our conditioning, and a common conditioning is that we do not believe that we have enough time, which often is a conditioned false truth that makes us choose to avoid taking hold of things. If you now want to create the life you want, you must be prepared to break this conditioning at any cost. It can feel like climbing a giant mountain, but without a strong desire to break your lack-of-time conditioning, you will be stuck in old patterns for life. This applies of course not only to time, but also to finances, health, relationships, and other issues. Your paradigm will always have excuses, so now you need to indicate that you have had enough of the excuses and actually are going to take hold of your life. If everyone did this, every diet and training program would work perfectly, but people do not do what they want deep down. Instead they do what their paradigm says, and the conditioning is defending itself to the last drop by bringing to life a variety of challenging feelings for us to overcome. Let us now once and for all create an action plan that takes you away from the conditioning, where you do not want to be. If you follow the exercise below, you will become more successful no matter what other things you do in life.

EXERCISE 12.4: *Plan for success*

1. What does your current schedule look like for a normal week? Draw up a chart on paper or in a program on your computer.

2. Divide the week into days from Monday to Sunday. Then divide each day in five parts: early morning, morning, afternoon, evening, and night.

3. Fill in all your planned activities and see where there is time left to implement actions that will help you take charge of your life and create the life you want.

Many people find when they do this exercise that they have free time, but the excuse of the time constraints is there to protect the conditioning that actually has been successful until now. You may argue that it has not succeeded, but that is not true; your paradigm has actually had its role until now. It will do everything possible to preserve the pattern that it has created for you to act according to its standards. Maybe it had to create a life full of restrictions so that you would get by, but it has worked. If you now are to create the life you truly desire, you must be willing to give up the conditioning that has been created with your soul blockages and wounds. You must also be prepared to derive and solve these conditionings' underlying causes with the Soulbalance method. Once you have got all this in place, you can write in your schedule all the things you should do to get your life as you want it. In most cases it makes no sense to delay work until the future, and a decision is enough to change your life right now. So why wait? You probably know that the longer you wait, the less likely it is that no change occurs. Take charge of your life now; there is nobody else who can or should do it. In isolated cases, maybe you have to wait because of an acute crisis that has to be resolved in order to be able to go on, but this is an exception and not the rule. The hardest part of change is not finding out where you want to be, for everybody can do that if they have the time and opportunity; the hardest part is to really make up your mind to create success regardless of external circumstances. If you have decided you must be prepared to go through your fears, become better at what you do, and you must be prepared for strong criticism from both yourself and others. Only then are you ready to achieve your dreams. We humans are creatures of habit, and your habit patterns like nothing better than to keep you where you are. People around you are also often comfortable with the person you are today, so even they will do everything to keep you from changing yourself, because it means that they must adapt, which is inconvenient for them.

You have probably worked with the exercise below earlier in the book. It is roughly the same now, but you are not the same, for you have developed, whether you believe it or not. Take the story of a girl who measures herself every day for a week to see if she has become taller. She will not see any difference at all. But eventually she may grow four inches in one year, which of course is pretty amazing. Why does she not see the change? It is too small to be discovered in a day, but in the long run it is great change. You may not yourself believe that you can develop so much in one day, but a small step each day will ultimately give you fantastic results. I myself am quite impatient and want to see quick results and sometimes wonder why no progress is made. But when I look back, the Soulbalance method cleared all my allergies, my phobias, my poor self-esteem, and so much more. Not bad for something that sometimes seems so subtle! The Soulbalance method is designed to help you heal and not to create sensational effects that give you a buzz for the moment. I have myself tried such methods, and they have never given me long-term healing, but only a short-term boost for the ego. Sure, you can reach the sensational things with the Soulbalance method, too, but if you are constantly looking for the thrill, then it is the ego that wants its attention. (See the previous section about the ego and how to solve these challenges.)

EXERCISE 12.5: *What can you now do to really take the step and realize your true self?*

1. Find out where you are concerning finances, health, relationships, or anything that feels important to you.

2. Find out where you want to be. Set a goal.

3. Your desire to achieve the goal must be stronger than the pattern or convenience that keeps you where you are now.

4. Establish an action plan.

5. Go ahead and make the change on the physical plane and go simultaneously through your fears and conditioned limitations. Dissolve them with Soulbalance method.

6. Develop and transform yourself on the way, so you do not hit your head against the same wall over and over again.

To go from Rough to Polished

If you start to dwell on the resistance and the adversity that you have encountered, it is important to realize that without them you would not be shaped in exactly the manner that will help you move on to where you want be. You are exactly where you should be, and you have been through what you should have been involved with so that you will now be able to grow into the person you always wanted to be. Without my enormous ailments, and my resignation, I would never have sought a solution but would have gone through life and just existed. Now I am thankful that my traumas connect me with the divine power that is there for everyone, but is ignored by many. I could not afford to ignore this power, for I was about to give up and leave this earthly life. So for me, the journey until now is exactly what I have needed.

Imagine you have a rough diamond that is huge. Without the enormous energy required to cut it, it would not have any value for those who want to wear it. Think of yourself as a rough diamond that has been gradually polished by various misfortunes. Now is the time for the diamond to be ready, so you can show off its beauty and share it with the world. Do you have the momentum necessary to really achieve what you want to have in life? Many people want a lot, but still sit in front of the TV or computer or have their hand in the cookie jar, without being able to accomplish something that contributes to taking them where they really want to be. To be able to go from your present situation to your dream location requires rocket fuel for your internal engine.

It is time to polish the diamond once and for all. How will you now be able to create the rocket fuel you need? There are four basic elements that create the momentum you need:

1. Fear
2. Pain
3. Love
4. Self-actualization

The first two create momentum, because most people want to get away from those states through a change, while love and self-actualization are what many want to achieve. Do you want to get rid of the fear and pain and strive to achieve more love and self-actualization? Then you have the rocket fuel that can help you create an active change and achieve your goals. I know that most of us have one or more of the four elements above and therefore we can create the rocket fuel necessary to change. There are two paths to follow: one path is that you want to get rid of something, and the other is that you want to achieve something. So it is open for everyone to change, not just those who carry grief and pain and not just for those who are in reasonably good balance and now want to fulfill themselves. It is so easy to fall into one of these categories, where you are either too ill to be healed or too balanced to develop. Through the Soulbalance method, all of us, and I do mean all, can grow into the people we are meant to be. Those who are satisfied with life as it is do not have the will and power to make the change. As I said, they are satisfied with the current situation, which is a goal in itself, and just right for them. These individuals are stuck until they have a goal they really want to achieve. Exercise 12.6 helps you really meet your limitations so you can achieve your goals.

EXERCISE 12.6: *Dare to face your limitations*
What is it in your subconscious that really restricts you from achieving your dreams? To find out, do the following:

1. Imagine that you take action and achieve all your goals. What kinds of resistance, negative thoughts, or feelings does this cause in you? Remember to look carefully, because these negative messages are well hidden.

2. Write down everything that comes to you in the form of restrictive thoughts, feelings, and so on. Make sure to let out what has lain hidden for many years, because it does more harm unconsciously than it does when you have identified the cause. Use the Soulbalance method for this step.

3. Keep in mind that this exercise is incredibly self-healing. But you must really confront what you have been hiding inside of you all these years for it to work.

But is this enough to get the results you want? No, unfortunately not. To obtain the results you want, you need:

• *Passion.* You really need to get involved in what you want, almost as a kind of love that you cannot resist. I really feel passionate about what I do. The people who I have helped and who get the most and best out of life develop a passion for what they do. You need to do something that you really want. The soul wants to help you get there.

• *Resolution.* Without really being sure that you will achieve your goals, everything you want remains an unattainable dream. The more you heal yourself with the Soulbalance method, the more the determination will grow within you. At first it may falter a bit, but the more confident you are of the presence of God in everyone and everything, the more you know you are in moving in the right *direction.*

• *Perseverance.* Make sure you are equipped with unlimited perseverance, because the major goals are blocked by obstacles that you must overcome. Almost everyone who is successful has almost given up at one point or another, but for some reason they have continued to fight towards their goals. I myself had not lived without my endurance, and this can even help you. You may say, "That I cannot do, I have no endurance," but endurance can be developed as most things in life, so just get started.

See how you handle these three points. If you have not got a grip on them, you will sooner or later give up your dream. Be strong and go through your fears with the help of the Soulbalance method to self-actualize what you want to do. Imagine you have a water hose and turn on the water with full pressure, yet no water comes out of the hose. Is the pressure wrong? No, the hose is full of junk which makes the water not able to flow. It is so with us humans. If there is a blockage or limitations, you cannot create success, no matter how much you try. The more you get used to transforming your limitations into opportunities, the more balance and success you will create.

Your inner Weather Rules

The weather is often dull in Sweden, but it is still "the inner weather" that controls how our life looks. Many people have an inner weather that constantly says too hot, too cold, too much sun, too little sun, and so on. Actually, their internal voice says that it is never something that is really good. These individuals often get undesirable results in all parts of life, not just in terms of weather, but also regarding finances, health, and relationships. Some complain and complain their negative internal voice cannot help but have its say, well hidden behind the weather. Stay far away from individuals who just whine and whine, which also attracts other whiners. If you are not careful you will be on their wavelength and begin slowly but surely take on their way of being, with direct or indirect negative effects. Stay away from external, negative factors that you still cannot influence. I have chosen to see the weather as positive regardless of whether it rains or is sunny, and what is funny about this is that my kids never whine over the weather. They are not conditioned to have a negative opinion about the weather. The weather is of course just as it is, but some of us have created an idea of what is good or bad weather. It is the same thing with our internal weather—we have often *learned* to create negative images of everything from health to finances and relationships. Here is an exercise that helps you free yourself from your bad internal weather, so you can create the life you really dream about. I really feel pain when I write about this subject, because until recently I lacked the power to self-create my inner weather. I now choose to do so – do you?

EXERCISE 12.7: *Transforming adversity into success*

1. What external circumstances drag you down? Write down these in a list.

2. Do you want to change what drags you down? Resolve the internal conflict with the help of the Soulbalance method.

3. Now change your negative thoughts to positive in those situations where you have let external circumstances control you.

4. See your improved attitude and your improved performance as a natural step towards better balance and success.

More on the law of Attraction

Similarity looks for similarity, all under the law of attraction. A person with poor finances often becomes a couple with another person with poor finances. Depressed people look for depressed people. We want help from those who have everything in balance, but do not seek contact because it costs a lot of energy. The solution is to dare to relax, to dare to dress as you want, dare to approach and talk to people you would like to know. For the law of attraction to work fully, you need to create balance and resolve your inner negative conditioning with the Soulbalance method. But this is not enough. You also need to ensure that you choose thoughts and activities that correspond to your newfound, positive, free soul. This can range from thinking positively about yourself to really realizing and doing what you have decided to do. With internal balance and external activity in line with your inner balance, the law of attraction will work for you.

Find Yourself by being true to Yourself

Be true to yourself. By being true to yourself, you will be able to create balance and move forward. To be able to live with your choices and know that you did right deep down inside you is extremely important. Live so that you on your deathbed can say you made the best of your life. Now imagine that you are lying there on your deathbed, knowing that you have not done what you were meant to do or really wanted to do in life. If you lived a life where you actually did what you were supposed to do, you will be in a completely different way open to proceed to the next life or dimension (a dimension is a time span between the different lives that vary in length, for God must find the perfect situation where you can be reborn, so that you get the soul development that you and your soul need).

Five pieces of advice to find yourself:

1. *Show inner humility; treat yourself with respect.* Many of us always try to treat others with respect, but unfortunately often forget the most important respect, which we all should show: self-respect. What is respect for yourself? It means that you do what is right for just you, not for anyone else. Sure, you can take advice from others, but you get the best self-respect when you become your own decision maker. If you have

self respect, you will finally make all major decisions within yourself with help of your intuition.

2. *Show external humility; treat others with respect.* The internal respect is superior to the external. When you have internal self-respect, respect for others will also grow. I do not mean that superficial respect where someone might say something positive, but not mean it, or really mean something negative. No, the external respect will come after years of training in internal self-respect. Note that the external respect is not about what others think you should be in order to be good enough in their eyes, but it is simply an extension of your respect for yourself. If you have respect for yourself and have freed yourself from all ego challenges, you will find that everything and everyone has the same value, but you do not have to like everything and everyone.

3. *Have an inner confidence that you will succeed in what you do.* If you continuously work on your relationship with God, your internal faith will also be strengthened. Your inner faith is an extension of the divine power that we all can have contact with. Your inner beliefs are much more than self-esteem. Your faith is your inner self-image in relation to everything created by God.

4. *Do what you shall and trust that God is there through thick and thin.* Surrender to the divine power that goes through you. If you do not believe in God, you can create things externally but you will still not experience balance. God is what gives us meaning at all times. When we

understand that we are an extension of God, all sense of meaninglessness can be resolved with the Soulbalance method.

5. *God does not need to prove himself or herself to us, but we need to prove ourselves to God.* Trying to prove God's existence is both impossible and negative, as belief in God is a nonscientific phenomenon that causes us to feel safe and have faith in what we do. The best results are created through an unlimited faith in the divine. There are four ways to boost that unlimited faith:

a) *Have faith in God.* Make sure that you trust God, as you will get so much more back. Your inner doubt makes you not get the results you should be able to get. This relationship is not there to put pressure on you, but it is a great tool to get us to rely on what is larger than ourselves. We are never alone; God is with us all the time.

b) *Have faith in God within yourself, the soul aspect.* While you have trust in God, you need to understand that God is there in your soul, ready to assist you so that you can do what you are meant to do. Your doubt about your capacity has always to do with your conditioning and can be solved with the Soulbalance method at all times.

c) *Have faith in evolution.* Remember that we are an important part of evolution and that our soul energy has been on this earth since time of the creation. The big bang theory as science claims is correct and explains how the world was created, but there is a greater intelligence that allowed it to happen. This intelligence, I choose to call God.

d) *Feel confident that the good within us and around us always wins.* The good will always prevail even though there is so much evil on our planet. The divine is a superior force compared with evil energy, so it cannot lose in the long term. But evil energy can cause short-term problems for us here on earth. Rely only on the knowledge that the divine always wins and God will show you the way.

"Be true to Yourself" contract

I have created a "be true to yourself" contract that makes it clear for you that you really want to focus on getting closer to your own truth. It is a commitment to yourself to really be true to yourself, so you can become the best you can and want to be, no matter what others think. The power of a written contract is the fact that you signed it, which is a far greater commitment than if the agreement is only in your thoughts. Take a contract for the purchase of a home as an example: Once you sign the purchase agreement, it is not only legally binding, but also an internal commitment to yourself. You have during the exercises trained yourself to make decisions based on intuition and to circumvent conditioned thinking by circling your intuitive decision with a pencil. Similarly, if you are really true to yourself, you can only sign a contract which is intuitively correct for you. Send yourself a letter in the mail containing the signed contract. You should put it in the mail and send it to yourself because we generally have a much easier time being accountable to others than to ourselves, because we believe that we must be good enough for others before we take care of ourselves. A contract in the mail is as if the contract comes from a third person, which increases the probability for you to really pursue your commitment. Once you have received the letter in the mail, read it again and then use it as a reference whenever you need.

"**Be true to yourself**" **contract**

1. I always follow my truth and nobody else's.

2. If someone tries to violate me and my inner truth, I will address the violation immediately, so that the violation has no negative effect on me. I act myself out of the offensive situation.

3. No one else can or should take responsibility for my life. I now take responsibility for my life 100 percent.

4. Adversity is only opportunity for development. I do my best to convert my adversities into opportunities.

5. I use my intuition to make decisive decisions in all situations.

6. I realize that my paradigm often makes me make decisions that are not true to me.

7. I have decided to only accept advice from and share my advice with people who respect who I am and what I do.

8. I have no duty to prove that I am good enough for someone else. I am good enough as I am.

9. If I end up wrong in life, I have the ability and the internal power to address and rectify this.

10. Nobody else has my ability to heal just me. I have decided to use that ability.

11. I am one with God, no matter what anyone else or my conditioning says.

Date and place

Signature

The Power of Affirmations when the soul blockage is healed

Affirmations are a very powerful tool if used correctly. When you work with affirmations, positive messages to yourself, together with solving the soul blockages, the affirmations create power and are able to assist you in the way you want. An affirmation used without resolving the soul blockages does not work for soul challenges, however much you may try.

Eleven Affirmations to use to develop Yourself

Use these eleven affirmations—that is, read them again and again three to four times per day for at least three weeks—and you will know that you really are a worthy person, which all people are. Then you will begin to heal yourself. Of course, you can replace one or more of the affirmations with others, but be aware that there needs to be power in what you read for it to have a positive effect.

1. I am good enough as I am.

2. I am good enough whatever others say.

3. I achieve what I want.

4. Nothing is impossible.

5. I am free from my internal and external criticism.

6. I love myself.

7. I value myself and others and have respect for life.

8. There are no limits to what I can achieve.

9. I earn the money I want.

10. I am one with God.

11. I am one with the universe.

Checklist to be Whole

Finally, I want to give you a checklist to be whole. You can check yourself anytime, anywhere, to see if you are on the right track.

Checklist to be whole

1. Realize that your parents' truth is not your truth.

2. Write down where you are regarding finances, health, and relationships.

3. Write down in the present tense where you would you like to be; let it flow freely. The difference between where you are and where you want to be creates anxiety and depression. These are just the external symptoms of the soul that tell you that you need to take yourself from where you are to your inner truth.

4. Write down a date for when your goal or goals will be met. If you do not have that focus, your subconscious will not understand that you are striving to achieve something.

5. Learn to communicate at all five levels. You may have a physical symptom that has to be resolved on the spiritual level, and you may have a spiritual message that you have to realize physically.

6. Find out what your limitations are. Feel them, write them down. Some things you are aware of; others you will just have an outer symptom to go on. Derive the underlying cause with the Soulbalance method and solve the blockages.

7. Decide to act so that you get your soul truth to the physical level.

8. Live your inner truth every day. Think about whether you live as you want or as others want you to live. If you live as others want for you, create change so you do not violate yourself.

9. Dare to develop and be the best you can at all times, no matter what your conditioning says.

10. Identify your need for control, and derive the underlying cause for it so you can release it. Dissolve the paradigms using the Soubalance method.

11. Make a change in behavior so that you go in a new, positive direction when you find the underlying cause.

12. Go through your fears. Dare to realize yourself, no matter how afraid you are.

13. Develop your intuition. It is your contact with the spiritual level where you can get all the information you really want and need. Create this contact with the help of the Soulbalance method. Finally you will dare to trust your answers.

14. Have faith in God.

Thank you for your time!

If you enjoyed this book and found it helpful, we would be so grateful if you could take a moment to share your experience by leaving a review. It can help us reach out to more people - thereby showing how we can use energy healing to heal blockages and reach our potential.

Follow our Newsletter and get your free spiritual Activation and E-Book.

Printed in Dunstable, United Kingdom

77378151R00161